C.W. ANDERSON'S COMPLETE BOOK OF HORSES AND HORSEMANSHIP

ALSO BY C. W. ANDERSON

Billy and Blaze
Blaze and the Forest Fire
Blaze and Thunderbolt
Blaze and the Gypsies
Blaze Finds the Trail
Blaze and the Mountain Lion

A Pony for Linda
Linda and the Indians
The Crooked Colt
A Pony for Three

Bobcat
High Courage
Salute
Big Red

The Horse of Hurricane Hill
Afraid to Ride
A Filly for Joan
Great Heart

Deep Through the Heart
Heads Up, Heels Down
Sketchbook

C. W. Anderson's
COMPLETE BOOK
OF HORSES AND
HORSEMANSHIP

with over fifty drawings by the author

THE MACMILLAN COMPANY, NEW YORK
COLLIER-MACMILLAN LIMITED, LONDON
1963

Library of Congress Catalog Card Number: 63–16746

Second Printing, 1964

The Macmillan Company, New York
Collier-Macmillan Canada, Ltd., Toronto, Ontario

Printed in the United States of America

Designed by Gertrude Awe and Jean Krulis

I have always felt that horses have as much individuality and character as people. The first horse I ever owned was so much of a person that ever since I have had difficulty in thinking of a horse as an animal. He was a big chestnut Thoroughbred, with a dark face and a crooked stripe. His name was Bobcat, and he was the most intelligent horse I have ever known. I feel that he understood everything I said, or at least what I meant. He was a real companion—more so than most people. He also had a sense of humor. Invariably, when I stooped over to clean his hoofs, he would take my hat in his teeth and toss it on the floor. Then up would come his head, with a glint of pure mischief in his eye. Part of the game was that I must pretend to be annoyed and scold him. If I failed to do so, he clearly showed his disappointment.

Bobcat was not a young horse when I got him, but his spirit was such that you would never suspect it. No matter how long the ride over the New Hampshire hills, he always went willingly and smoothly. Even coming back from a ten-mile ride, he would go into a long, swinging, sustained trot so rhythmic it was something to dream about. Much of the country was rough and stony enough to call for a walk, but a walk bored Bobcat. He developed a smooth jog that ate up the ground and was so springy it was a delight. That was many years ago, but I still remember that gait with a glow of pleasure.

He had a ten-acre pasture, but I never had to go and get him. One call, although he knew it meant work, and he would come galloping to the barway at top speed. When he opened up it was really something— and it made you realize what a handful he could be without his manners. But he always gave you only what you asked for. I have never known a truer gentleman.

So this book is for you, Bobcat.

CONTENTS

ILLUSTRATIONS

THE ORIGIN OF THE HORSE

Archeologists tell us that the horse preceded man on earth by many ages, but scarcely anything is known of its history earlier than 2000 B.C. What little we know, we learned by studying the fossil skeletons found deep in the earth. Those judged the earliest were found in the Mississippi Valley area of the United States.

These early skeletons show that the *Eohippus*, from which our present-day horses descended, was no larger than a fox and not unlike him in conformation: short-legged and with toes instead of hoofs. His development was slow. We have evidence that a larger species of wild horse, the *Mesohippus*, was plentiful in the Stone Age and was hunted for food. The Mesohippus was about the size of a sheep and thousands of these skeletons were found stacked in front of a large cave near Lyons in France.

It was in areas where vegetation was rich and plentiful that the Mesohippus thrived and grew in size. In remote parts of western Mongolia a small scrubby horse is found today, so stunted in growth that he is little larger than his toed ancestors. Intensive inbreeding and scant forage are obviously responsible for this arrested development.

Further proof of this was found in the Grand Canyon. On a high plateau, isolated and all but inaccessible, a band of horses was discovered in 1940. How they got there is not known, but it was obvious that they had been there a long time. Inbreeding and scant food had stunted them until they were less than half the size of their mustang forebears.

Aside from the fossils, the first visual proof we have of the horse's existence on earth is in the prehistoric caves of France. There, drawings on the walls, primitive as they are, distinctly depict the horse—smaller and shaggier but unmistakably the forebear of the horse as we know him. Later, in 4000 B.C., the Assyrians, in sculptured reliefs, show horses not unlike those depicted by the Greeks in their marbles.

The Greek horse as seen in the Parthenon frieze and other ancient sculpture was very compact and round-bodied with little indication of wither or backbone. Since the Greeks rode bareback this was the most comfortable type of mount and what they tried for in their breeding. Judging by the sculptures, the Greek horse had much of the high, spirited action of our gaited saddle horse and an even higher carriage of the head.

When the horse first became the servant of man he was probably no more than a small shaggy pony, for in remote areas of the world where he has been left to shift for himself he is still that. Care, good feeding, and, most important, selective breeding started the horse on his way to being the large powerful animal we know. The breeder's axiom "breed the best to the best" must have been understood even in those far-off days.

"Wherever man has left his footprint in the long ascent from barbarism to civilization we will find the hoofprint of the horse beside it," wrote a noted archeologist. Truly the history of man is so dependent on the horse that it could not be written without him. The figure of man on horseback was a symbol of power from time immemorial. The ancient Greeks had almost as great an admiration for the horse as for the human figure and lavished loving care on their carvings of both.

The horse was unknown in America when the Spanish conquistadors first set foot on these shores. Their conquest was made

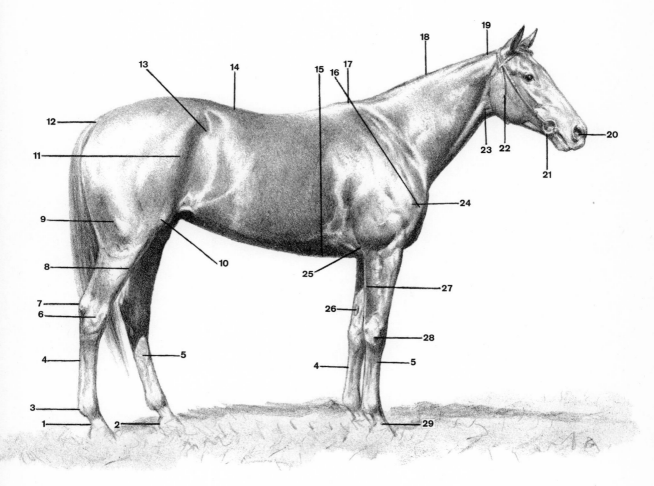

A horse's anatomy

1. Pastern   2. Heel   3. Fetlock   4. Tendon   5. Cannon   6. Hock   7. Point of hock   8. Gaskin   9. Thigh   10. Stifle   11. Quarters   12. Dock   13. Hip 14. Loins   15. Depth through heart   16. Slope of Shoulder   17. Withers 18. Crest   19. Poll   20. Nostril   21. Chin groove   22. Jowl   23. Throatlatch 24. Point of shoulder   25. Elbow   26. Chestnut   27. Forearm   28. Knee 29. Coronet

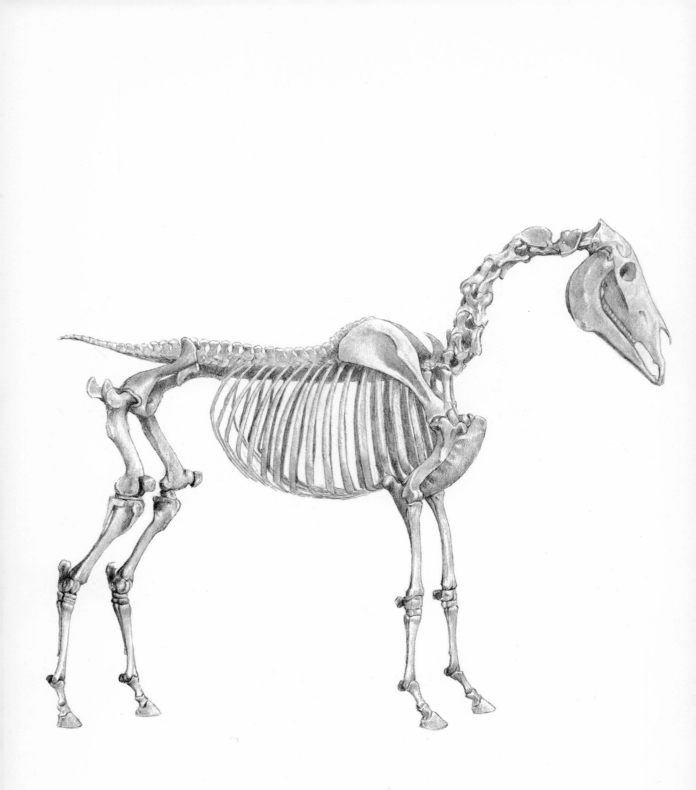

A horse's skeleton

easier, since the Indians were terrified at the sight of the Spanish horses. They had never seen such creatures. The Spanish horses were of Arabian and Barb blood and were noted for their toughness and endurance. It was from a handful of these horses, which escaped or were stolen by the Indians, that the western plains were eventually populated with herds of wild horses. Caught and broken by the Indians and later by the white man, they became the bronchos of the vast cattle lands. That they inherited the toughness and durability of their Spanish forebears has been proven time and time again.

In the earliest days the Moors and Arabs did the most to improve the breed of horses. Crossing Arab and Barb blood with the best of native stock, they obtained so fine a type that it aroused great enthusiasm in the Crusaders of the twelfth and thirteenth centuries. Many of these horses were bought and taken back to England. Although they were too small to carry a knight and his full armor, they were in great demand for pleasure-riding. When the discovery of gunpowder made lance and armor useless, they came into their own. Their blood was very important in building a foundation for the Thoroughbred yet to come.

When we consider all the varying breeds and types of today, it seems scarcely believable that they all stem from the small Mesohippus. The diminutive Shetland pony, scarcely larger than his remote ancestor, and the huge Percheron, weighing the better part of a ton, are brothers if we look back far enough.

Horsemen in each field have established an ideal type and try to breed true to it. A pony should not be too big or he might lack quality, a Thoroughbred not too small or he cannot carry weight. A definite uniformity is desired in each breed, but requirements differ in accordance with what the animal is expected to do. A

A horse's muscles

gaited horse must have high, flashy action or he will be considered useless in his field, while the race horse and hunter must have a reaching stride with no waste motion. The harness horse should know only the trot or pace and never gallop, but the gallop is the natural gait for the Thoroughbred, Arabian, and cow pony.

It is little short of miraculous that from a single source could come such a variety of individuals with such different capabilities. Among wild animals there is always a general uniformity in size and physical ability. There is no such range in any species as that between a child's pony and the huge Percheron, no such speed variant as that between the small gallop of a Shetland and the blazing drive of a race horse. Only selective breeding for centuries could have achieved such results. Most horses can jump obstacles three feet high, but exceptional jumping ability must have existed on both sides of the family to produce a Heatherbloom or a Great Heart capable of jumping eight feet! All horses love to run and use such speed as they possess, but what a far cry from the scamper of the little Eohippus to the gigantic stride of a Man o' War or a Native Dancer.

Size, of course, evolved gradually as the centuries passed, but growth was augmented greatly when man began weeding out the poorer specimens and breeding the best to the best. In medieval times, large powerful horses were necessary, for a knight in armor weighed a full four hundred pounds. Henry VIII decreed that all stallions, except ponies, under fifteen hands in height should be destroyed. This concentration on size helped develop the huge eighteen- and nineteen-hand draft horse. With the discovery of gunpowder the armored knights disappeared. Then the accent in breeding was on speed and handiness, and the huge chargers were relegated to more menial tasks.

This sketch is a copy of one of the paintings found in the Lascaux Caves in Southern France; archeologists date them from the last Ice Age. It is clear that the horse, in small form, existed in those far-off days.

From then on the purpose of the breeders was to produce a useful horse, for it was man's only means of conveyance and his travels were limited by the quality of his mount. It was at this time that the great influence of Arabian blood took hold, for the knights had brought back many Arabians from the Crusades. Although they were too small to carry a knight in full armor, they were ideal as all-purpose horses. The stage was now set for the advent of the Thoroughbred and the many other breeds that owe a debt to him.

THE BARB AND THE ARABIAN

The Arabian, smaller than the average Thoroughbred, is seldom over fifteen hands in height. He is very compact, with a short back, an arched neck, and a notably fine head carried high. The jowls are wide and the head tapers to a fine muzzle. Seen from the side, the line of the nose is slightly concave. The nostrils are very full and flaring, and the eyes are large and expressive. Great width between the eyes is characteristic, always a sign of intelligence. Quality is everywhere in evidence in his conformation.

The color of Arabians varies: chestnut, gray, bay, or brown, rarely black, and never spotted. A full flowing mane and tail are characteristic.

In the earliest days Arabians were decidedly smaller than those of today, twelve to thirteen hands as a rule, with fourteen being exceptional. Obviously, here, as with the Thoroughbred, selective breeding has increased the size of the Arabian. The Barb has always been interbred with the Arabian, so they are closely related. Spain imported many Arabians and crossed them with her native stock to produce fine horses, much sought after by other countries. The Spanish horses painted by Velásquez, a master draftsman, show a very powerful, compact horse with much quality and the Arabian blood very much in evidence.

The early Arabians were also brought into Macedonia and Greece, and the horses seen in Greek sculpture show unmistakable signs of Arabian blood. In fact, the Arab and the Barb are responsible for all the breeds we now have, from the small pony to the massive draft horse.

Quality is apparent in this Arabian stallion. It is easy to see that he is the forefather of the Thoroughbred.

The Barb originated on the Barbary Coast of North Africa, noted as the home of the Barbary pirates, who preyed on the world's shipping in other days. The Barb horse, however, is all virtues and no vices. So closely related to the Arabian in conformation and temperament is he that there is no doubt they have the same antecedents. The Barb was much used in mountainous country and thus developed what the natives termed "goat feet." He will climb steep inclines, travel along narrow paths at dizzy heights, and never have a mishap.

The French have a native cavalry regiment, the Seventh Spahis, all mounted on magnificently trained Arab-Barb horses. On command these horses drop to the ground and thus form a shield for their masters, who lie prone to fire over them. In two World Wars they have given outstanding service and suffered incredibly heavy losses. They more than held their own against the world-famous Uhlan cavalry of Kaiser Wilhelm, all mounted on stallions, considered much braver than geldings for the work they had to do. (These horses were also trained to defend their masters, rearing and striking with their forelegs and biting when possible.) On Bastille Day, when the grand parade comes down the Champs Élysées with the Seventh Spahis, turbaned and with flowing white cloaks over scarlet vests, the horses all but dancing to military music, the cheers are overwhelming. The pride of each man in his mount is communicated to the crowd.

In North Africa the Barb is still raised with utmost care of selection and occasional infusion of pure Arab blood; hence, he is finer in quality than ever. As a cavalry horse he has been considered supreme. It is said that he can go farther with less food, rest, and water than any other breed except, possibly, the pure Arabian. In temperament he is completely reliable and exceptionally cooperative and intelligent.

The great sensitivity and intelligence of the Arabian shows clearly in its head.

These traits are also present in the Arabian. He is capable of carrying one-fourth his weight, which would be upward of 230 pounds, no small feat for a fifteen-hand horse. Having lived in the desert and endured its heat, he can go indefinitely without water and perform prodigious feats of endurance with little or no nourishment. Under all these conditions he will go willingly and never at a sluggish pace.

The fact that an Arab treats his horse as a member of the family and usually has him sleep in the tent has made the Arabian feel extremely close to man. A British officer who lived many years in the desert said that never in all that time had he seen a single ill-tempered or vicious Arabian horse. Perhaps this gentleness was explained when the officer said that the Bedouin performs feats of horsemanship and control of his mount with a bitless bridle that a dragoon could not equal with a strong bit.

Another British officer, with years of experience, states that he has known Arabian horses to be ridden continuously for forty-eight hours over the hot sands without food or drink, and still go on willingly. Such performance would seem fantastic, but many others have verified this. He further said, "They have a delicacy, I cannot say of mouth, for it is common to ride them without bit or bridle, but of feeling, and obedience to the knee and thigh, to the slightest check of the halter and the voice of the rider, far surpassing what the most elaborate *manège* gives the European horse, though furnished with snaffle, curb, and all."

Another British officer and noted horseman gave perhaps as good a description of the highest type Arabians to be found—the Nejeds, considered the purest of all Arabian strains. This was in 1865 and in the part of Arabia noted for the quality of its horses. He wrote, "Never had I seen or imagined so lovely a collection.

Their stature was indeed somewhat low; I do not think any came up to a full fifteen hands, fourteen hands seemed about the average, but they were so exquisitely shaped that want of greater size seemed hardly a defect. Remarkably full in the haunches, with a slope of shoulder so elegant as to make one, in the words of an Arab poet, 'go raving mad about it,' a broad head above, tapering down to a nose fine enough to verify the phrase of 'drinking from a pint pot,' a most intelligent and a singularly gentle look; full eye, sharp thornlike little ear, legs that seemed made of hammered iron, so clean and yet so well twisted with sinew; a neat round hoof just the requisite for hard ground, the tail set on, or rather thrown out, at a perfect arch, coat smooth and shining, the mane long but not overgrown, and an air that seemed to say, 'look at me.' "

In the early days of English fox hunting, a Mr. Childe originated a new style in hunting by riding straight to the line of the hounds, taking the obstacles as they came. He went at such a pace that he was nicknamed "Flying Childe." He had acquired a gray Arabian as a hack, since he considered him too small to hunt such a "big" country as the Quorn. On trying him out he found that the little gray was superior to anything in the countryside, and for many seasons he and his Arabian showed the way in the most competitive hunts. The little horse was noted not only for his jumping but also for his light way of galloping over "deep" ground without sinking into it. For this reason his owner named the horse Skim.

Despite many tales about the fleetness of the Arab, speed is not his forte. It is his endurance, quality, and disposition that set him apart. He can do many things well, and always does them willingly.

THE THOROUGHBRED

Sometime around 1690 three extraordinary horses were imported into England. The first was known as the Byerly Turk; it is not certain whether he was of Barb or Arabian origin. In the fourth generation his line produced Herod, one of the foundation sires of the Thoroughbred.

Next to arrive was a horse known as the Darley Arabian. He was a bay horse of about fifteen hands, which was large for an Arabian in those days. From his line, also in the fourth generation, came Eclipse, regarded as one of the greatest stallions that ever lived.

The third of the trio that was to bring the Thoroughbred into the world was the Godolphin Arabian, and there are so many conflicting stories about him that his origin is the most uncertain of the three. From him, in the second generation, came Matchem.

To these three—Matchem, Herod, and Eclipse—every living Thoroughbred traces in direct male line. It is hard to get an idea of what they looked like, for the camera was not yet known and the artists of the period had such a stylized way of depicting the horse that any individuality failed to come through. In fact the proportions and conformation they showed are unlike those of any horse with which we are familiar. All the points admired in that day were exaggerated beyond recognition; the quarters were tremendous and heavily muscled, as were the shoulders, topped by an extremely slim, swanlike neck. The head was made unbelievably small, obviously to show fine blood. The spindly legs and pasterns depicted would never have supported that overmuscled

Stymie, inbred to Man o' War, had that great horse's high-headed imperiousness.

body. However, it is safe to assume they were not unlike our present-day Thoroughbred, although probably smaller, for it is known that Thoroughbreds have increased in size even in the last decades.

Matchem was said to be a rather common-looking horse that matured late. He failed to win a single race in his first two years of competition but was never defeated thereafter. Our own Fair Play line, which gave us the mighty Man o' War, traces back to Matchem and has the same characteristic late maturity. However, they did not inherit their progenitor's looks, for all the Fair Plays are strikingly handsome.

Herod and Eclipse were never beaten, certain proof of their exceptional class. It is very rare for a horse to have such consistency that he remains unbeaten throughout his career, or even through a single season. These three had every right to found a dynasty that reaches to all corners of the earth.

As a performer, Eclipse was the greatest of the three. Not only was he unbeaten—he was absolutely unbeatable. The only way that the owner could get a wager on his horse was to stipulate that Eclipse would outdistance his rivals at the ratio of sixty yards to the mile. Even under these conditions he rarely lost a bet.

A wit of the day wrote a verse which became very popular.

> *Eclipse, all nags compared to thee,*
> *Excite contempt and laughter;*
> *There never was a horse, I do*
> *Believe, so much run after.*

In any list of great horses, you always find Eclipse at the top—not only because he was the first of the great ones; by his record alone, he belongs at the top. A horse that so outclasses all his rivals has to be truly great.

They seem to run in threes, these foundation sires, for in this country we have our American lines of Domino, Ben Brush, and Fair Play; their blood shows in the pedigrees of nearly all our horses. Domino and Ben Brush are descendants of Eclipse; Fair Play, of Matchem.

All Thoroughbreds are registered: a complete chart of breeding as well as color and markings is put on record. Without such registration a horse is not allowed to race. This is to keep the bloodlines pure. Crossing a Thoroughbred with cold blood may produce the calm temperament wanted to make a quiet hack or hunter, but speed is lost, and speed is what a Thoroughbred is raised for.

To a large extent, development of all other breeds stems from Thoroughbred blood. The trotter and pacer are a cross of Thoroughbred with mares that showed a liking for the harness horse's gaits; the three- and five-gaited saddle horse is also that cross with mares who had high, flashing action under saddle. The quarter horse of the West is Thoroughbred blood on the quick-breaking cutting horse, which starts and stops on a dime. It has been found that Thoroughbred blood added both speed and stamina to the cow pony, and many Thoroughbred sires are now sought for breeding in the cattle country of the South and Southwest.

The average Thoroughbred is fifteen to sixteen hands in height. A hand is four inches and the measurement is taken at the withers. Horsemen like to see their colts grow to a good size. Fifteen hands is considered small for a mature horse; something nearer sixteen is preferred. There have been many fine racers that were on the small side, but they are obviously under handicap when matched with larger horses with a longer stride. Man o' War, who was over sixteen and one-half hands, had the longest stride ever seen on the track; at full racing speed it covered twenty-five feet.

Clearly the only chance a smaller horse would have against him was to stride more quickly and this none was able to do.

However, most horsemen prefer a medium-sized horse, between fifteen two and sixteen hands. A majority of our best have fallen in this category. Still we occasionally have a "king-size" one that is also good. Omaha, who won the Derby, Preakness, and Belmont, to enter the very select circle of Triple Crown winners, towered above his adversaries, standing close to seventeen hands under the standard. Generally, though, such size is a handicap on the race track. A very large horse lacks the handiness required on the turns and, if knocked off stride in close quarters, is slow to recover himself. He is usually slower at the start and is not able to take advantage of an opening as his smaller, quicker adversaries can. Some horsemen feel so strongly on this point that they refuse to buy a horse over sixteen hands in height.

In every instance when Thoroughbred blood has been used as a cross with another breed there has been improvement in quality. In polo, where speed and cleverness are imperative, it is the Thoroughbred pony, or the one that is nearly so, that is supreme. No Western cow pony can match strides with a quarter horse, which has a strong strain of Thoroughbred blood. The speed of the Arabian has been hailed in song and story, but the fact is that, though this blood is the fountainhead of the Thoroughbred, the finest Arabian is no match for a third-rate Thoroughbred on the racecourse. In the hunting field, when the pace is hot and the point long, it is the man mounted on the Thoroughbred who is in front. It was a noted fox hunter who said, "A drop of blood is worth an inch of bone."

All Thoroughbreds have their birthdays on the first of January regardless of when they were foaled. This is to avoid complications in grouping them for racing. Two-year-olds racing against each other may vary in age as much as six months, but generally the variation is not so great. Breeders like to have their foals arrive early in the spring so they are at least nine months old on their first birthday. On rare occasions a breeder may over-reach himself in his eagerness to have an early foal and have his colt arrive a day or two before the first of the year. According to Jockey Club regulations this foal would be a year old when he is barely able to balance on his shaky legs. The breeder saves himself (and racing officials) embarrassment by keeping the foaling date secret until after the first of January.

Before the youngster goes to the races he must be given a name. This is no easy matter, for many thousands of names have already been used and there can be no duplication. Besides that, a Jockey Club rule says that a racer's name must not exceed sixteen characters, including spaces between words; a trotter's name, ac-cording to a U.S. Trotting Association rule, cannot have more than twenty characters, including spaces. The ideal name will give an idea of the breeding of the colt or filly and also have color and interest. For example, it would take no Sherlock Holmes to guess that Crusader, American Flag, Battleship, and Hardtack were sons of Man o' War.

Since a youngster is still an unknown quantity it would be risky to go in for too much grandeur in a name. Indomitable would be an unfortunate choice if the colt proved to be faint-hearted. Still, the horseman has to take a chance. He would not want to have a Derby winner named Pete or Joe. But rarely has a good horse had a poor name. Perhaps the owners have second sight—they might have seen something in the youngster that made them take a chance on a name that would fit a champion.

In the list of winners of our most famous stakes there is no Pop's Pick or Gottawin or Kumarunnin. The Belmont Stakes, perhaps the most searching test for three-year-olds, has a roster of winners whose names ring out like a bugle call. There is Ruthless, Hastings, Commando, Colin, Hourless, Man o' War, Crusader, Gallant Fox, War Admiral, Whirlaway.

Perhaps the outstanding characteristic of the Thoroughbred is pride. It is this fiery spirit that keeps him going when a cold-blooded horse would drop. That very fine race horse, Dark Secret, met with disaster in his final appearance on the track. Under a furious head-and-head struggle through the stretch, he was seen to bobble and all but go down, then recover and come on again. By some miracle of courage he held on right to the finish line. Then it was discovered that his leg was so badly fractured that he had to be destroyed.

The blood runs hot in the Thoroughbred and the courage runs deep. In the best of them, pride is limitless. This is their heritage and they carry it like a banner. What they have, they use.

THE MORGAN

One of the most popular breeds stems from a single foundation sire of unknown origin. A small, compact, bay stallion named Justin Morgan had such prepotency as a sire that those bearing his blood a century and a half later are unmistakably stamped with his characteristics.

Justin Morgan was named after his owner, who bred him primarily as a riding horse. He was foaled in 1789 in West Springfield, Massachusetts, and later moved to Randolph, Vermont. There are no pictures of him in existence, except word pictures that are definite enough to establish his type.

"He was a dark bay, without a white hair on him, standing fourteen hands and weighing 950 pounds," writes one observer. "He had a lean, intelligent head, a kind eye, large nostrils, and a tapering muzzle. His back was very short and he was noticeably strong through the loins, very powerful in the chest, short-legged with very good clean bone.

"He was a fast walker and his trot was low and smooth. He did not raise his feet high but he never stumbled. Under the saddle he was very obedient and responsive, almost anticipating your desires. He was gentle and kind to handle and loved to be groomed, which showed in his sleek coat, very noticeable in those days."

He was a fleet runner and was raced often. These impromptu races were at sixty rods, approximately a quarter of a mile (the distance of our quarter-horse races). He was rarely beaten and

A young Morgan colt

the countryside always enthusiastically backed him against all comers.

Horses were used to pull logs out of the woods, and there were often arguments as to who owned the stronger horse. Pulling contests arose from these arguments, similar to those so popular at country fairs in years past, except that logs were used instead of a stoneboat loaded with granite. The report is that Justin Morgan was never beaten in these contests.

Although little is known of his breeding, it seems certain from the description of him that he must have had considerable Arabian blood. In disposition also he seems to have had much in common with the Arab. Today, however, the Morgan is considered an American breed and the greatest efforts have been made to keep true to the ideal type. For a time some breeders were crossing Morgan blood with Thoroughbred and saddle-horse strains in an attempt to get more size, but they soon found that when they departed from the true type they lost character and performance. Evidently his handiness, toughness, and endurance depend on the balance that the true Morgan has. When these breeders got a taller, leggier horse, they lost much in performance. They learned that he was at his best if left as he was meant to be: compact, rather short in the leg, and with great power in the loins and quarters.

Horsemen consider it a mark of quality in a stallion if he definitely *stamps his get;* that is, passes on his own characteristics and conformation to such a marked degree that his offspring can be readily identified. In this the Morgan stands alone, for he breeds truer to type than any other breed. Thoroughbreds vary a great deal in size and conformation, even those by the same sire. Man o' War was a big horse, standing a full sixteen hands and three inches, yet two of his best sons, War Admiral and Battleship, were on the small side, being more than a hand under the size of their sire. There is no such variation in the clean-bred Morgan, but rather an amazing uniformity in size, conformation, and all characteristics.

As a pleasure horse he is ideal, for he performs equally well under saddle or in harness. Most Morgans have enough aptitude at jumping to make especially good children's hunters. They are the right size for youngsters and are free of the stubbornness that is often a characteristic of ponies. Also, they are up to much more weight than might be expected, and unless a man is built on a very large scale the Morgan can carry him over long distances with the utmost willingness.

Morgan Clubs are found all over the United States, and a National Horse Show exclusively for Morgans is held each year— usually in Vermont, where Justin Morgan spent the greater part of his life. In this hilly and even mountainous terrain, the Morgan comes into his own. Sure-footed over the roughest going, he proves the right horse for the adventurous rider who likes to leave the beaten path and explore. It is in this area that the annual Hundred Mile Ride is held. The event is open to all horses, but it is usually the sturdy offspring of Justin Morgan that are showing the way. Endurance and a toughness that provides considerable immunity to lameness are two of the qualities that make this breed so popular with those who know it.

Both armies used many Morgans in their cavalries during the Civil War. It is said that the mount Sheridan used in his famous ride was a Morgan. The first stanza of "Sheridan's Ride," the famous poem about the exploit, concludes, "And Sheridan twenty miles away." That seems the sort of job a Morgan could do.

This is the type of conformation desired by most breeders of Morgans: on the small side but very compact and powerful.

For many years the United States Army maintained a farm in Vermont where they had stallions that traced in direct male line to Justin Morgan. Mechanization of the army came, with elimination of the cavalry, and with it the passing of the most dashing and picturesque branch of the service. The sturdy little horses are now really pleasure horses.

THE SADDLE HORSE

There is probably no horse that has more dash and style than the five-gaited saddle horse. His walk is regal and his trot, with high, proud head and bold, piston action of knees and hocks, is poetry itself. Yet it is when the cry "Let them rack" is heard in the show ring that everything else is forgotten. This is the gait for which the horse is famous.

The gaited saddle horse is an American breed. The early colonists depended on a riding horse for transportation, for the roads at that time were mere rough, rutted trails and rarely fit for carriages or wagons. For covering long distances, a smooth, easy gait was a great asset. Naturally, horses that possessed such gaits were the ones most highly prized, the ones chosen for breeding. The improvement was so pronounced that by the time Arabian and Thoroughbred blood was brought in, a type was already established. The infusion of Arabian blood gave increased stamina, beauty, and intelligence. Thoroughbred blood increased the size considerably, possibly as much as a full hand in a century; it also added fineness of line and greater speed. Morgan blood, introduced later, gave added sturdiness and adaptability, qualities for which this little horse is noted. Thus, the modern American saddle horse is a cross of three outstanding breeds of the equine world.

The gaits of the three-gaited saddle horse are the walk, trot, and canter, executed with high, spirited action. In the five-gaited we add the rack and the slow gait. The primary requisite for a gaited horse is high, true action. It is so different from that

The five-gaited saddle horse seems all style and fire, but he has plenty of stamina.

of the Thoroughbred race horse and the cow pony, who lift their feet just enough for clearance, that it is obvious the greatest care in selection has been taken for generations to "set" the type.

Kentucky and Tennessee produced the first American saddle horses. One of the most famous of the early sires, and one that might be called the foundation sire, was a horse named Tom Hal. He was bought in Philadelphia and ridden by his new owner to Lexington, Kentucky. If further proof was needed of the durability and stamina of this stallion, it is on record that he covered a distance of eighty miles in one day and made the return journey the following day. He lived to the unusual age of forty-one years, and it is from his blood that the great saddle horse sire Bourbon King was bred.

Another famous name in the history of the American saddle horse is a horse called the Stevenson Mare. Bred to the noted stallion Denmark, she produced Gaines Denmark, whose name appears in the pedigree of most of the best saddle horses. In 1908 the American Saddle Horse Breeders Association officially designated Denmark as the foundation sire of the American saddle horse. He was a Thoroughbred and it was through his mating with the Stevenson Mare that he became so important to the breed. The Stevenson Mare was of old colonial stock. That she was an exceptional horse is apparent, for in her son Gaines Denmark she got a horse so prepotent that he passed on to his offspring, almost without exception, the qualities that have made the American saddle horse what he is today.

If a horse is destined for the show ring, an operation on the tail is necessary to give the high *set* required in these classes. Also, a longer toe and heavy shoe are used to get higher action. With so much flash and style the gaited saddle horse may seem something of a prima donna, but he has plenty of rugged endurance. When competition is very keen in a class he may be asked to go at his best pace for an hour or more. It is doubtful if many horses of other breeds could match that for sheer endurance.

There are many great names on this breed's roster of champions, and one of the greatest is Wing Commander. This brilliant performer won the Grand Championship Five-gaited Stake in Kentucky for six successive years. He had great beauty and a style that was unforgettable. Other famous names are Lady Carrigan, Chief of Longview, Garrymore, and My Show Boat.

The Tennessee Walking Horse is a cross of Thoroughbred, Standardbred, Morgan, and American saddle horse. Allen F 1, a Standardbred, was the first great stallion of the Tennessee Walking Horse. He was brought to Tennessee in 1891. His son Roan Allen is said to be the foundation sire of the modern walking horse.

This horse was developed primarily for use on large plantations, where an easy comfortable gait was essential to the planter who spent most of the day in the saddle. Although the Tennessee Walker has a good canter, it is his running walk that he is noted for. At this pace he can cover six to eight miles an hour so smoothly that the rider might think he was in a rocking chair.

In common usage a saddle horse means a pleasure horse or a hack. He can be of any breed, size, or color; the paramount thing is that he have smooth gaits, good disposition, and, above all, willingness. A western horse often makes a good hack, for he is used to long hours under saddle and is sure-footed. The one drawback is that he may lack a good trot, for it is a gait not used with a western saddle. His canter, called a *lope* in the West, is very smooth and can be sustained over long distances.

The Tennessee Walker covers a lot of ground with this flowing, comfortable gait.

A Thoroughbred has all the qualities to make a fine hack if he is not too hot; if there is any sign of competition he can be quite a handful and a mount for only a seasoned rider. Often the half-bred makes a more dependable hack for the average rider. The usual combination in breeding is a Thoroughbred sire and a mare that has a little Thoroughbred blood.

A hunter usually makes a good hack, for he is used to looking out for himself over all kinds of terrain. If you are in an exploring mood, there is the added advantage that a log or ditch will not stop him. The Arabian makes a fine mount, for his gaits are smooth and his disposition and willingness are exceptional. His canter is his finest gait and he can maintain it indefinitely.

The Morgan is also a good horse under saddle—tough, willing, and kindly. He is on the small side but so sturdy he can carry more weight than might be supposed. He lacks the long swinging trot of the hunter and Thoroughbred, but he is ideal for a youngster and is very popular as a lady's horse.

The dressage horse can be of any breed but is usually a Thoroughbred or a saddle horse. He can perform amazing feats in intricate maneuvers, work so involved that only a highly intelligent and obedient horse could master it. Dressage training calls for the greatest patience on the part of both horse and rider.

The cob, more common in England than in this country, is a rather small chunky horse that can be used for both hacking and hunting if the fences are moderate. He is very rugged and up to a lot of work.

The requirements for all horses under saddle are different, but in one essential they are the same. George Washington, expert horseman, said it all when he declared, "What I ask of a horse is that he will go along."

THE WESTERN HORSE

The western horse can be of any blood or breeding and usually is a cross of many. The distinguishing mark is that he is ridden in a western saddle with a high pommel and a horn used when roping cattle, and with a bridle that has a single rein. The mustang of the early days was a descendant of the wild horses that roamed the plains and foothills of the West. These can be traced back to the horses of the Spanish conquistadors. The Spanish horse, a cross of Barb and Arabian blood, set the pattern for the mustang. Since that day much other blood has been introduced, notably Thoroughbred and Morgan. The best gait of the western horse is his easy canter—the lope. This he can maintain over great distances, for this horse is noted for his endurance and toughness. He can stand up under all-day work with only grass for nourishment.

A cutting horse must have speed and great flexibility, for he must be able to outrun and turn the animal singled out and keep him from rejoining the herd. This is no simple task, for a steer, despite his ungainly appearance, is capable of great bursts of speed. He must also have as much knowledge of cattle as his rider, and once shown the animal desired, stick to it like a burr.

Much the same sort of requirements are needed for a good roping horse. He must have the speed to stay with a calf or steer and know what position to be in to give his rider the best chance with his loop. Once the animal is caught, the horse must keep the rope taut until it is tied. All this requires alertness and a high degree of intelligence. A well-trained cow pony knows range work as thoroughly as any cowpuncher. So highly prized is a good cutting horse or roping horse that he commands thousands of dollars, although an ordinary one can be bought for a few hundred.

Thoroughbred blood is becoming more and more important in the West, mostly through the quarter horse, which is not a breed but individuals selected because of early speed and quickness in starting. They are usually at least half Thoroughbred, and many are full Thoroughbreds of sprinting blood. Since the races for these horses are, as the name implies, at a quarter of a mile, sprinting sires are the ones used in breeding quarter horses.

The quarter horse is very compact with tremendously developed quarters. The shoulders are also very powerfully muscled and the barrel is big. The whole body seems to bulge with muscle and even the novice can see the tremendous power this horse has. His blood is highly prized by cattlemen, for speed and quickness are essential in working with cattle.

The rodeo horse is also a specialist, but of a far different kind. He is usually the outlaw who will not be broken. He has a single-track mind and it is devoted entirely to devising new and more violent means of ridding himself of anyone who gets on his back. Almost all western horses buck when being broken, and when one shows up that is unusually bad and shows no sign of changing, he often ends up in the rodeo, where his special talent is wanted. Some of these outlaws become famous, or at least notorious, for their sheer orneriness.

When one of these buckers throws a top rodeo rider, he is on his way to a reputation; if he throws the cowboy with the wide belt signifying the championship of the world, he is famous in rodeo circles. These horses soon learn all the tricks there are to

The rodeo horse is usually a chronic outlaw, but sometimes he is just an extraordinary athlete capable of amazing bucking acrobatics.

unseat a rider and seem to constantly invent new ones. Only sinews of rawhide and steel can stand the violence of the action and the bone-crushing impact of landing. The nerves must also be of steel, for riders have been killed in rodeos and many seriously injured. It's just about the toughest way imaginable to make a living, but these game, hard-bitten men would probably be bored with an easier, less dangerous life.

Cow ponies come in a wide range of colors, much more varied than the Thoroughbred. What is called a skewbald or piebald in the East is a paint or pinto horse in the West. The strangely spotted horse called the Appaloosa was much admired by the Indians, and most of their mounts were either paint or spotted horses. It is written in old tales of the West that many tribes traded off or ate all the solid-colored horses that they bred or caught or stole. The varicolored came to be called Indian horses, and even after the warlike tribes had been subdued and banished to reservations, there remained a prejudice against the Appaloosa and paint horses because they brought back memories of many a bloody massacre.

Palaminos are not a breed but a type, or perhaps it is better to say a color. They are in great demand as parade horses, particularly in the West, for their golden color and flaxen mane and tail are very showy and striking. They seem to sense the admiration of crowds, for they carry themselves in such a proud, high-headed manner. The ideal palomino is one with a coat the color of a newly minted gold piece and a full, flaxen mane and tail. The type originated in Mexico in the 1800's, where a large ranch devoted itself exclusively to the breeding of palominos. This involved considerable experimenting, for the color does not often breed true when palomino is bred to palomino. The offspring usually has a lighter coat and a light eye, both of which are undesirable. The most successful method is to breed a chestnut stallion to a white or near-white mare. Even then the occurrence of true palomino color in the offspring is less than 50 per cent.

The western horse in general is tough, durable and intelligent. He can forage for food and water and take care of himself. Unless crossed with other blood he may not be much for looks, but he makes up for this in performance. He can go over trails that would be highly dangerous to other horses. When horsemen speak of a *using horse*, they are describing him.

HORSES IN HARNESS

The Hackney, a smart horse or pony in harness, is not a breed but a type, bred by the English for a spirited gait. Good knee and hock action are wanted, plus high, proud carriage of the head. In 1822 some were imported into the United States and their blood was used in breeding American trotters. Most horse shows have Hackney pony classes and they are very popular, for this little fellow has a gaiety, dash, and verve that always captivate the crowd. The Hackney really knows how to put on a show.

The huge draft horse, later used as a work animal, was originally bred to carry the knight in armor, no small task. In 1217 a hundred stallions of the Percheron breed were imported from Normandy to England. All over Europe the emphasis at this time was on size rather than speed. The Dutch and Flemish horses were large, as were the Clydesdales of Scotland and the Shire and Suffolk punch of England. The Belgian was known as the "Great Horse" of medieval days; seventeen to eighteen hands in height and weighing up to 2200 pounds, he was docile, willing, and very powerful.

The Percheron originated in Le Perche, Normandy. The head, unlike most draft horses, is small compared to the body, a definite Arabian trait. They show other Arabian characteristics, for they are quicker and more agile than most of the other heavy horses.

The Clydesdale, bred near the river Clyde in Scotland, is slightly smaller than the other horses of this type, with a higher action at the walk and trot. He has much style and his blood has

The trotter's action is the same as that of a Thoroughbred's trot but he is capable of much greater speed. The action is on the diagonal, the near forelegs and the off hind legs in unison.

been used in the past to get a big powerful coach or carriage horse.

The Shire horse is native to the middle section of England, the famous hunting country. He stands higher than the others, often reaching close to twenty hands, and is characterized by a very full, hairy fetlock (called by the English, with typical understatement, *feathers*) that often almost hides his hoof. His blood, crossed on Thoroughbred in England, has produced heavyweight hunters that can carry upward of 20 stone, or 280 pounds.

In America the day of the draft horse is over. Even the die-hard farmers who loved their matched teams have had to surrender to the tractor. There was a time when one of the really blue-ribbon events at the country horse shows was the pulling contest, with great draft horses hauling stoneboats loaded with unbelievable weight in granite blocks. They were the greatest attraction at the show or fair. Now they are gone.

Until the time when the automobile took over, nearly everyone had a horse. Two centuries ago, most roads were merely rugged trails, fit only for horses under saddle. The popular races in many parts of the country were trotting races, but under saddle. This was the beginning of a sport that was to cover the country. Since travel at that time was over great distances, the trot rather than the gallop was the gait most used, and it naturally followed that racing should be at this pace. Later, in the horse-and-buggy days, every man had pride in his "road horse," and impromptu races resulted any time anyone attempted to pass the vehicle ahead of him. Masculine pride in the speed of his transportation was as great then as now—probably greater, for the pride a man feels in a fine horse cannot be felt in the same measure for a machine, no matter how fine its performance.

The nineteenth century was the time when thought was given

The Shire stallion is typical of the huge, powerful draft breeds.

to breeding for greater speed. More careful selection of the best individuals resulted in speed never before realized. Formal racing also began, and in 1806 a horse named Yankey trotted a mile under saddle (on a half-mile track at Harlem, New York) in 2:59, which was then a record. This is a far cry from the two-minute mile now achieved by our best horses. Some of this great advance can be attributed to better tracks and the greater speed possible in a light sulky, but not all of it. Much of it must be credited to selective breeding, the basis for improvement in all breeds.

Harness racing soon followed, with a high-wheeled, rather heavy cart. In 1885 Maude S trotted a mile in 2:08¾, which was then deemed the ultimate in speed. It was argued that a two-minute mile was an utter impossibility. Probably, under the racing conditions of the time, it would have been.

There are two gaits in harness racing: the trot and the pace. The trot is a natural gait, the near foreleg and the off hind leg striding in unison. The pace (the legs on each side go forward almost in unison) lacks the fluid grace of the trot, but it has a great speed potential.

The bicycle sulky was introduced in 1892, and with its advent new records appeared. Lou Dillon was the first to reach the supposedly unattainable goal of a two-minute mile. In 1903 she trotted a mile in 1:58½. The legendary Dan Patch was the first pacer to cover a mile in two minutes. These two were real heroes in their day. No gathering place for horsemen was complete without colored prints of these great horses in full stride.

Most of the horses racing at that time traced back to two stallions: Messenger, who died in 1808, and Justin Morgan, who died in 1821. Messenger was an English race horse, imported

Greyhound, one of the greatest trotters that ever lived

with the idea of improving the running horse, but his offspring showed an inclination to trot. Hambletonian, a descendant of Messenger, had such a vogue that for a while he quite over-shadowed Justin Morgan. But horsemen soon realized their mis-take in neglecting the blood of that sturdy little stallion, for he contributed much in the toughness and *bottom* (stamina) so necessary to a harness horse.

Although in the early days there was much diffusion of blood in the harness horse, it is Hambletonian, the great-grandson of Messenger, and strongly inbred to him, that is considered the foundation sire of the Standardbred, and most of them trace back to him.

In the earliest days races were held at distances of up to one hundred miles. The A.S.P.C.A. was instrumental in stopping such marathons, and before long the mile was accepted as the stand-ard distance, as it is today. The sport has grown tremendously in popularity, and in addition to the tracks devoted entirely to harness racing, most race tracks have meetings for the trotters as well as for Thoroughbreds.

With racing and breeding on such a scale, it is only natural that records do not last too long. There are new heroes every year, but some of the older ones are still remembered. Dan Patch, that great pacer, is still a legend, as is Lou Dillon. The time they made on those old tracks, with sulkies far inferior to those of today, points them out as truly great.

Possibly the Man o' War of the harness horses was a big gray gelding named Greyhound. He so outclassed all of his opposition that in the latter part of his career he had to run exhibition races as none could be found to oppose him. In 1938 he trotted a mile in the record time of 1:55⅘. His stride was so long and smooth that he seemed to float over the ground. The turf writers called him the "Gray Ghost." He was one of the truly great ones; many called him the greatest.

Harness racing continues to gain in popularity all over the United States, as it should, for a good horse extended in a trot is a beautiful sight. It is the gait our forefathers loved, and it must still be in our blood.

PONIES

To qualify as a pony, the animal must be under fourteen hands two inches. Greater height makes him a horse by American show-ring standards. Other countries have different ideas. In the famous Leicestershire country of England an animal under fifteen hands two inches is called a pony. The Lamb, a famous steeple-chaser that twice won the Grand National, was a pony to English horsemen. He stood a bare fifteen hands two inches, which makes his achievement all the more remarkable. Many a powerful seventeen-hand chaser has found those tremendous fences too much for him.

On the other hand, the standards in Devonshire are totally different. Here, from the earliest days it was decreed that a pony should be under twelve hands. Anything larger is considered degenerate, brought on by some cross on the ancient Exmoor blood.

"Strictly speaking, a pony is one of a tribe reared for generations untold on mountains and moorlands, without shelter and without other food than natural herbage," wrote a noted English horseman in the late 1800's. "The true pony is bred because nothing of greater size can be reared under the circumstances of soil and climate."

The Shetland pony is probably the best-known type, and because of his small size is a great favorite with children. He originated in the Shetland Islands, where soil and climate made it impossible to breed an animal of any great size; the sheep and cattle there are much smaller than elsewhere. It is thought that his ancestors were the Norwegian ponies which he resembles—

the island was long a part of the Scandinavian kingdom. The natives of the Shetland Islands prefer a pony not over ten hands, and many are less than that. The Shetland is very sturdy and surprisingly strong for such a small animal. He was always useful as a beast of burden, but in 1840 he came into even greater demand to haul coal over the tramways in the coal mines. Boys did this work until a law was passed forbidding the use of boys as "beasts of draught." Once ponies were put to work in the mines they were kept there, and few ever again saw the light of day. The work was hard but they were well fed and well cared for.

A famous breed of ponies, the Exmoor, originated on a twenty-thousand-acre tract in Scotland leased from the crown by Sir Thomas Acland in the early 1800's. This rugged and forested terrain was used for breeding ponies and sheep. In such all-but-impossible footing, the Exmoor became as sure-footed as a mountain goat and could gallop down the steepest incline without a stumble.

The Exmoor is larger than the Shetland, running upward of thirteen hands, and is very compact and muscular. An old English book relates that a twelve-hand Exmoor stallion jumped a thick five-foot stone wall with ease. Most of them are natural jumpers, though not quite up to such a feat. If purebred they retain their characteristics and size; crossed with Thoroughbred blood they may gain as much as a hand in height.

Welsh ponies, like the Shetland and the Exmoor, subsisted in the earliest days on what they could graze on the moors. When crossed with Thoroughbred blood, they have gained substantially in size. Many believe, however, that something is lost when a pony is bred to a greater size than has been characteristic for hundreds of generations.

The Shetland pony is a great favorite with children, especially when he is as sensationally marked as this one.

Another breed, the New Forest pony, was originally just what our wild horses of the West were—the offspring of indiscriminate and unplanned breeding. As a result they came in all shapes and sizes, for they ran wild through the rugged countryside of southern England.

The rough terrain of Dartmoor has produced yet another breed of ponies. The Dartmoor has survived in a rock-strewn countryside that offers the poorest of forage and natural shelter. The size preferred in the Dartmoor is twelve and a half hands, but the Dartmoor ponies are often under that. Unusually strong, they can carry a man if asked to. As a child's pony they are excellent. Their heritage from their early hardships is a tough durability and absolute sure-footedness. They are long-lived, a pleasing quality in a family pet.

The Highland pony is a native of Scotland, and as with many pony breeds, his origin is lost in the mists of the past. They run in height from twelve and a half hands to fourteen and a half. They are fine riding ponies, for they are strong, docile, and very willing. These ponies are also used by deerstalkers in the Highlands, and they can carry a deer weighing two hundred and fifty pounds over the roughest terrain.

The Hackney pony, a small edition of the Hackney horse, is the old type, and there is uncertainty about its origin and bloodlines. A small horse called Sportsman, foaled in Yorkshire a century ago, seems to be the foundation sire, for there is no previous record of a horse of this sort. The Hackney pony must have the ultimate in action, the knee almost touching the muzzle in his pistonlike stride. This pony is rarely seen except in the show ring, where he is very popular because of his great spirit and style.

Of late years a breed of ponies from the west coast of Ireland has caught the public fancy as no other has. The Connemara rightly deserves such popularity, for in addition to a perfect disposition he is sensational as a performer. In the show ring he has proven that he can hold his own against top horses in jumping classes.

Until 1900 the Connemara was a wild pony that had to fend for itself under difficult conditions. It was not until 1928 that the Connemara Pony Breeders Society was formed for the preservation and improvement of the breed. It was decided to keep the breed intact and avoid crossbreeding with outside blood. This policy and selective breeding have made the Connemara what he is today: in the opinion of many horsemen, the outstanding pony in the world.

The origin of the Connemara is lost in the remote past. It is believed that he might be a mixture of Highland, Shetland, Icelandic, and Norwegian strains, with the wild horse of Mongolia as his remote ancestor. All evidence indicates that the Connemara pony is the oldest equine inhabitant of the British Isles.

A Connemara standing a mere thirteen and a half hands won the jumping championship at Madison Square Garden in 1939. In doing this he beat a field of jumpers that so towered over him that he seemed a child's pony gone astray. He was the famous Little Squire, the most popular horse in his day. He could jump higher than seven feet. Of him, Danny Shea, who owned and rode him at the start of the pony's American career, said, "He was not only the greatest jumping pony in this country, but he could jump any kind of fence that a top horse could jump. He didn't care if it was the widest or the highest; he would try anything he was asked."

Another famous Connemara, The Nugget, jumped seven feet

Here is a pair of Connemaras, mare and foal. Although small enough to qualify as ponies, they are more like small Thoroughbreds in conformation.

two inches. He was undisputed champion in England and Ireland and won three hundred prizes in his career. He was big for a Connemara, standing fifteen hands, but was classed as a pony by the European standard.

Still another Connemara, Dundrum, is current favorite and champion in Europe. He has jumped six feet five and is probably capable of more height. His greatest asset is that he will face anything, no matter how strange or large, with supreme confidence. An admirer who knows Dundrum well says of him, "Although he has the courage of a lion he is as gentle as a lamb." More can scarcely be said of any horse.

Over a hundred pony clubs are active in the United States and the number is constantly increasing. Even in this motorized age, the pony has held his own.

BREEDING AND BLOODLINES

Although Thoroughbred breeding is sometimes called a science, there are plenty of instances when it seems like the wildest game of chance. Even the time-honored maxim of "breeding the best to the best" is not infallible. Two plus two does not always make four, and too often has a disheartening way of adding up to zero.

From the 1880's, when Bruce Lowe figured it out most scientifically with statistics and charts (which often turned on their creator, tripping him up time and again), to the present, nothing very tangible has been certain except that a good sire and a good mare often produce good horses and that a poor sire and a poor dam seldom do. Even this obvious generalization becomes a bit shaky when we remember that McGee, a sire of mediocre sprinters, sired Exterminator, greatest stayer of his day, perhaps of any day.

These are the exceptions, however, and the sires that lead the list of winners are almost invariably horses of fine breeding that were outstanding performers on the track. Racing is the testing ground, and the weak and unfit are weeded out there more stringently than in any other sport. A horse that won't fight when challenged in the stretch will not be given a chance to pass on his lack of heart.

A good sire and dam will quite consistently produce good-looking, well-made colts and fillies, but in racing this is not enough. No matter how fine his conformation, how smooth his way of going, if he is a second or two under racing speed he is worthless in that field. Often, however, he may be made into a fine hack or hunter or even a steeplechaser, where such a high turn of speed is not required. Two of Man o' War's sons were failures on the race track, but when trained to jumping were outstanding. The handsome Holystone, hunter champion of some years ago, was all but unbeatable in the show ring, and gallant little Battleship, winner of England's famed Grand National at Aintree, had no competition "through the field." They failed to inherit the blazing speed Man o' War so often passed on to his sons and daughters, but enough quality came through to make them champions in other fields.

There is some difference of opinion among horsemen about the relative importance of the sire and dam in transmitting quality to a foal, but the general opinion is that the dam is the more important. It has been pointed out that a top mare has produced stakes winners when bred to a number of different sires. This can be explained by the fact that only the finest performers are put to stud, so a breeder might choose any of a score of stallions and not go amiss if his mare has quality. Even the finest stallion has little chance of getting anything worthwhile if bred to mediocre mares.

An exception to this was that great red horse Man o' War. All through his career, his "book" of mares was so lacking in quality that no breeder with a top stallion would accept them today. Yet from such material he sired some of the best horses of his day. His own quality was so great that the fact that there was little for the foal to inherit from his dam made hardly any difference. He stamped most of his get unmistakably with his high-headed imperiousness and fire, regardless of the characteristics of the mare.

For a time great faith was placed in *nicks:* combinations of bloodlines that seemed to have great affinity for each other. Fair

The feminine look is not hard to see in these yearling fillies.

Play and Rock Sand was a famous nick which produced Man o' War and other good ones. This worked, it might be noted, except when poor daughters of Rock Sand were bred to inferior sons of Fair Play. Similarly, the famous Domino-Broomstick nick was successful only when both sire and dam were fine individuals. When the qualities of the sire and dam supplement each other, as in this instance (Domino was a sprinter and Broomstick a stayer), the reason for the success of the combination is apparent. In fact it seems clear that a nick is merely a combination of blood-lines where each individual contributes qualities that the other lacks.

Some breeders who have tried to accentuate certain qualities have resorted to inbreeding. This is breeding a sire to a dam where each has the same blood in its pedigree, usually rather close up. The most extreme example we have was the sprinter Ultimus, who was by a son of Domino out of one of Domino's daughters. Since Domino was speed incarnate it was easy to see what was hoped for. Ultimus had speed, but the close inbreeding shortened his tether and he was more limited in distance than his sire or dam. Such close inbreeding is usually a dangerous practice, for faults are more often amplified than quality and disposition often suffers.

One shining contradiction to this ordinarily correct conclusion was the fine stayer Stymie. Both his sire and dam are out of Man o' War mares. This is very close inbreeding, and particularly so when it was to the fiery, tempestuous blood of Fair Play. One horseman said that it was like trying to put out a fire with gasoline. Yet Stymie was no more difficult than most highbred horses and better than many. Of him, his trainer said that it was only when he was "good" that he was tough. When he was all wound up and ready for a top effort he had a chip on his shoulder and was hard to handle.

Sometimes a stallion seems to transmit more qualities to his fillies than to his colts. In such cases he is known as a brood-mare sire. Such was the case with Man o' War. Although he had many brilliant sons, among them War Admiral, one of the finest of his day, still his fillies were outstanding as brood mares. Even those that were failures on the track were often wonderful when returned to the breeding farms. The fact that they seemed all but worthless on the track did not prevent them from passing on some of Man o' War's great qualities to their foals.

Kelso, voted the horse of the year in 1960 and one of the really great performers of recent years, is an interesting example of this quirk in inheritance. His sire, Your Host, was definitely a sprinter and was unable to handle the mile and a quarter of the Kentucky Derby; yet his son Kelso is all but unbeatable at any distance. Two miles is the same to him as six furlongs. Looking at his pedigree you feel that this stamina has to come from his dam, for seldom does the sire contribute more than he himself has. When you see that Maidoduntreath, by Man o' War, was his granddam, you need scarcely search farther for the source of his stamina. Even though she was not much as a race mare, she must have passed on more than she herself had. One of the great old-time horsemen said, "The Man o' War mares are a law to themselves."

If breeding were a cut-and-dried affair in which the results of each mating could be figured out mathematically and precisely, it would be far less interesting than it is. The very fact that quality, perhaps even greatness, can come from unexpected sources gives hope to the modest breeder who cannot afford the huge stallion fees of the popular sires. Alsab, one of the truly

The great mare Busher and her first foal

great horses of the last two decades, was by an obscure stallion out of a ninety-dollar mare. So the little horseman can still dream. If it happened once it can happen again.

Horses are brothers and sisters if they are by the same sire and out of the same dam. Horses by the same sire and out of different dams are no relation to each other according to breeding standards and usage. Those out of the same dam but by different sires are half brothers or half sisters. This ruling may at first seem arbitrary and illogical, but when you realize that a stallion may be bred to forty or more mares a year, it is easy to see why the ruling was made. Otherwise the breeding picture would be cluttered up with so many half brothers and half sisters that the relationship would be meaningless.

There is almost invariably a tremendous difference between horses that are full brothers or sisters. The same cross of bloodlines only rarely repeats itself in quality and performance. Time and again when the brother or sister of a great horse has appeared in the sales ring, the bids have been tremendous, but none has even approached its illustrious relative. In fact, most have been downright failures. One exception that comes to mind is that of the three brothers Gallant Fox, Fighting Fox, and Foxborough. Although the older brother, Gallant Fox, was by far the best, the other two were good, consistent stakes winners. Strangely enough, these same bloodlines again produced brothers that were of top quality. When Gallant Fox was put to stud, he sired Omaha and Flares, both racers of the highest quality. Omaha won the Triple Crown, a rare feat, and Flares won the famed Ascot Gold Cup.

The breeding of a horse is given in the form of a chart so you can readily see just what combination of blood produced him.

As an example the pedigree of Man o' War is given below. The top name in each bracket is the sire and the lower one the dam. He was by Fair Play out of Mahubah, who was by the imported Rock Sand. An asterisk always indicates an imported horse.

Fair Play was a fine race horse and a great sire, although criticized by some because of his fiery temperament. This he inherited, though fortunately in a lesser degree, from Hastings. Fair Play was fiery and impetuous, while Hastings was downright dangerous. Fair Play's son Man o' War was not of his temperament, but there was plenty of dormant fire there. Of him you could well say, "Handle with care."

MAN O' WAR
Chestnut,
1917

- FAIR PLAY
  - HASTINGS
    - SPENDTHRIFT, BY AUSTRALIAN
    - CINDERELLA, BY TOMAHAWK OR BLUE RUIN
  - *FAIRY GOLD
    - BEND OR, BY DONNCASTER
    - DAME MASHAM, BY GALLIARD
- MAHUBAH
  - *ROCK SAND
    - SAINFOIN, BY SPRINGFIELD
    - ROQUEBRUNE, BY ST. SIMON
  - *MERRY TOKEN
    - MERRY HAMPTON, BY HAMPTON
    - MIZPAH, BY MACGREGOR

When all is summed up, the breeder is most intent on choosing a stallion that seems most likely to provide qualities his mare lacks. If she is temperamental he must be careful not to breed to a very high-strung sire, for temperament is the trait most likely to be inherited. If she is small-boned he will probably choose an unusually rugged stallion in hopes of correcting this weakness in the offspring. A mare that lacks stamina should, of course, not be bred to a sprinter; for in doubling up that blood you are apt to produce a colt with too short a range for even our shortest races. On the other hand, stamina bred to stamina can sometimes produce a plodder, too slow to win at any distance.

In short, what every breeder really wants is a horse that can sprint with the sprinters and stay with the stayers; a Man o' War, an Exterminator, a Kelso. All he needs is a fine mare, a great stallion, a lot of patience, and all the luck in the world. Or maybe a little more than that.

THE FOAL

For the first few days it may be said that the foal casts no shadow of his own—he is so close to his dam at all times. This is partly due to the timidity of a small creature in a large strange world, but he also wants to be close to the source of supply, for his appetite is great and continuous.

It is best if from the very first he is accustomed to being handled by men, for then he knows he has nothing to fear from them. Therein lies the difference in breaking a hand-raised colt, such as the Thoroughbred, Arabian, Morgan, and saddlebreds, as opposed to the western horse. The cow pony has scarcely more contact with man in his earliest days than the wild mustangs that roamed the plains. Consequently, in order to save time, force is used to break him.

Xenophon, the great general of ancient Greece, stated the horseman's creed as well as it has ever been said: "See to it that the colt be kind, used to the hand, and fond of man." There have been many great trainers whose precepts would fit into that sentence.

Since the Thoroughbred foal is so highly bred, he might well be used as an example. All that is asked of a foal at first is obedience. This is very essential, for before too long this fuzzy, leggy youngster will weigh close to a thousand pounds, and what could a hundred-and-fifty-pound groom do to control him if he has not learned obedience early.

At first mares and foals are kept in small separate paddocks, for often there is jealousy, and heels are in evidence. Later, when they are sturdy enough to look out for themselves, a number of mares and foals are turned out together, and then begins the romping and playing that will make up so much of a foal's early life. There will be impromptu races—mad dashes around the paddock, with the mares joining in. It is amazing to see these spindly-legged youngsters not only keep up with the pace but often outrun their mothers. Stablemen keep a sharp eye on these paddock races, for very often a fine horse has his speed from the very beginning and his superiority shows early.

With Thoroughbreds, little halters are put on early, usually in a week or two, or a month at most, and they are taught to lead. The more they are handled at this age the better mannered they will be later. A good groom can instill so much training in his handling of foals that breaking them is very simple, seemingly only another step in the daily routine.

Mares and foals at pasture are like youngsters at school; before many days they begin to pair off, each apparently finding a particularly congenial spirit in the group. Janon Fisher, the Maryland horseman who won nationwide acclaim by training the Man o' War jumper Blockade to win three Maryland Cups, observed that mares and foals of the same breeding will usually pair off and stay together. Out of a group of more than a dozen yearlings turned out on his farm, two by War Admiral were always found side by side, and they had to be brought in together or there was trouble. Apparently they inherited enough similarity of taste and temperament to be particularly congenial to each other.

Within the first few months the foals will develop enough individuality so you can get some idea of the sort of horse you will have at maturity. A strong straight leg with good bone will already be in evidence, even though the legs are so long and slim

During the first days the foal is completely dependent on its mother.

Although well grown the foal still likes to be close to mother.

in relation to the body. If it is to be there at all, the sloping shoulder, so highly prized, will show early, and the points that will insure strong quarters and clean hocks can be seen by the experienced horseman. What a thrill when he sees in his paddock a small replica of a great horse he once raised—the same bold, questioning eye, the same air of confidence, almost arrogance, and again that long, swinging stride. It must be the same thrill the old prospector felt when he saw the glint of a nugget in the bottom of his pan.

Many people, outside the Thoroughbred breeding areas, speak of all young horses as colts, but in a horseman's terminology a colt is a male horse under five years of age and a filly is the female counterpart. Youngsters of both sexes are foals until they reach the age for weaning. Then they are called weanlings, and later yearlings. After that, they are colts and fillies and after five they are horses and mares.

Although a foal will nurse until weaned, it usually begins to show curiosity about the food its mother eats fairly early. It is a common sight to see a leggy youngster spreading his long legs as far apart as possible to get down to try the strange green stuff his mother finds so satisfying. But grain is usually more tempting, and he will often share his dam's feedtub. Soon he will have his own feedbox.

At as early an age as three months the youngsters have very definite characteristics, although they may all look pretty much alike to the casual observer. An experienced horseman, however, can often walk into a paddock of foals and with amazing accuracy name the sire of each, although he has never before seen any of these youngsters. The heads in particular, immature as the foals are, often have a definite resemblance to the parents at least for those who are trained to see.

In color a foal may take after either of his parents, or be a compromise between them. If either is gray the foal is pretty apt to be that color. Some stallions transmit their own color to a great degree, regardless of the color of the dam. Such are called *dominant* for that color. A vast majority of the Man o' War offspring inherited his chestnut coat. If the sire or dam has a blaze and a white stocking or two, all of the offspring are apt to be well marked with white.

The coat of the Thoroughbred ranges from black (which is not too common) to the lighter bay and brown. Bay is seen most often, and there is an occasional roan, a combination of chestnut and gray. Skewbalds (a coat part bay or chestnut and part white) and piebalds are rare among Thoroughbreds. The pale golden color of the palomino is almost unknown.

A patch of white in the middle of the forehead is called a *star;* a wide band of white from forehead to nose is a *blaze.* A narrow band of white is a *stripe*, and a small patch of white at the nostril is a *snip*. These markings grow in size with the growth of the foal, but never change in shape, and they are used for identification.

As the time approaches for the youngster to be weaned he has already shown that he is no longer dependent on his dam. He spends much more time away from her side, playing with his fellows, and when turned into the paddock it is often the son that leads the way while the mother follows. He is a big boy now and gone is the remembrance of his complete dependence on his quiet, patient mother. He is sure of himself, even a bit arrogant, in his new-found strength. Only when darkness closes in does the desire to be close to his mother's side reappear. With the first morning light his confidence and self-sufficiency are renewed. He is growing fast now.

One day in the fall the foal's routine is changed. Instead of being led to his old box stall he is taken to a distant stable and put into a separate stall. Then ensues such a chorus of shrill, heart-rending whinnies as to try the hardest heart. Actually he no longer is at all dependent on his dam, but a lifetime habit is not easily broken, even though the lifetime is a very short one. The mare is again in foal, and after the first brief agony of her loss, she is again the placid expectant mother, while the foal soon forgets his dam.

The thoughts of youth may be "long, long thoughts," but the memory is very short. Glorious days of play and grazing in the broad green paddocks with youngsters his own age will erase the memory of his early days so completely that he may pass his mother without even recognizing her. Fortunately she also has other interests now, so suffers none of the pangs of the mother who cannot adjust to her offspring's self-sufficiency.

There is nothing better for a growing colt than to romp, play, race, and fight a bit with his fellows, even if it gets a little rough. They are now rugged animals and often a cut or bruise comes from these exuberant scuffles; but if a colt is kept to himself he may become timid and horse-shy, and thus be at a disadvantage on the track, where he must never flinch at being in close quarters.

Many horsemen claim that it is a mistake to look at a foal with too critical an eye until it is a month old, for many seeming faults are outgrown by then. Pasterns that at first seemed too long and sloping have become stronger; knees that were sprung will become straighter.

The old adage that a foal's legs are as long at birth as at maturity is, of course, an exaggeration, but they do appear inor-

Even at this early age, character is already noticeable.

dinately long for that small body. Even at six months the body has not caught up with the legs, but a trained eye can be pretty sure of what will develop. The only trouble is that fine conformation and fine performance do not always go together. Count Fleet, one of our truly great horses of the last two decades, was faulted by all horsemen as a two-year-old, and these faults of conformation must have been even more pronounced when he was younger; but there was no horse of his day that could match strides with him.

Growing colts are like growing boys—their appetites seem out of all proportion to their size. Although they may be out at grass for the greater part of each twenty-four hours, they also get eight or ten quarts of oats and are usually looking for more. All this nourishment is not going to waste, for these weanlings now weigh five hundred pounds and stand upward of thirteen hands. They still have to gain another five hundred pounds and almost a foot in height before they are mature, but they are well on their way and many of them already look every inch the race horse.

The fillies have their own paddock and they are a lovely sight. Immaturity seems to sit more gracefully on the gentler sex, and their deerlike slenderness and feminine heads give them great charm. Their eyes are different from the colts'—gentle and slightly timid; whereas the colts already have a bit of fire in their expression. An experienced horseman can usually tell the colts from the fillies merely by the expression seen in their eyes. Although some great race mares have been amazons, the masculine-looking ones have rarely made good brood mares, so horsemen always like to see their fillies definitely feminine in appearance and the colts masculine. The great ones have usually fitted into this pattern.

This weanling filly is like a teen-ager—not a child and not yet a woman. In six months she will have nearly grown up to her long legs.

Still there is nothing so definite that we can become too arbitrary in matters of conformation and characteristics. The fine ones do not always fit the pattern. Some have seemed common on the outside that had greatness within. The great Exterminator was so angular that he was called "Old Bones." Perhaps it would be best to follow the old horseman's precept and look first and longest at the eye. The story is often there.

INTELLIGENCE

Discussions about the intelligence of the horse have been frequent, and there is a wide divergence of opinion. There is the hard-boiled viewpoint that the horse is a dumb brute and must be forced to obedience at all times without any nonsense. Another, and it includes a surprising number of seasoned horsemen, insists that horses are intelligent and much can be done without force. They feel that reason can often be used with a horse as successfully as with a person.

A well-known writer of dog stories insisted that the horse is the stupidest and most cowardly of animals. Such a viewpoint is so at variance with the observations of men who have spent their lives with horses that it must be based on ignorance and a complete lack of contact with the horse. You can no more know if a horse is clever or stupid when you have no understanding of his nature or reactions than you can know the mentality of a person if you do not understand his language.

The question must be considered from the standpoint of a horse's instincts. In his wild state, like the deer and the antelope, he relied on speed to escape his enemies. The fact that he will shy or run from some trivial thing, some small animal one-tenth his size, does not prove that he is either a fool or a coward. It is a purely instinctive reaction, carried over from bygone ages when he was smaller and even more helpless. A dog, on the other hand, being a carnivorous animal, has the instinct to attack rather than flee. Yet a horse, when handled with understanding, can be taught to overcome his natural timidity if he has full confidence in the person handling him.

A good memory is considered a mark of intelligence, for the dolt forgets almost at once. A horse never forgets anything. It is doubtful if even the vaunted memory of the elephant can surpass his. For example, a horse was ridden along a road he had not seen for years. At one point he became very nervous and shied violently for no apparent reason. Only later was it recalled that three years before he had been very startled when a cluster of white rocks beside the road suddenly became a group of squealing white pigs.

A horse will never forget a road or path he has once known, even though it is overgrown and all but obliterated. A place where a partridge suddenly let go with his feathery thunder will not be forgotten and that spot will always be looked at with suspicion.

He can communicate with you to an amazing extent if he sees that you understand him. You may pass the stable and see him look at you and then turn his head to the corner of the stall where his water bucket is located. If you investigate, and finding the bucket empty, refill it, he will always tell you in this way that he is thirsty. If he keeps turning his head back to you when you are riding, it is best to investigate, for you can be sure something is amiss. I have known a horse to turn and bite the toe of the rider's boot to let him know that something was twisted under the saddle and hurting him. The extent to which a horse can communicate with his owner depends almost entirely on the perception and understanding of that person.

A horse's intelligence is different from that of other domestic animals. He has dignity and reserve. You must win his confidence over a period of time before you get anything approaching affection. Dogs will often fawn over anyone for attention and petting, but the horse is no pushover to be won by sweet words and mere gifts. He must know you for a long time before he accepts you. Then he is no fair-weather friend.

In the 1930's at Madison Square Garden, a Major Tuttle performed intricate maneuvers, far beyond the "high school" routines of dressage, on Thoroughbreds that he had taken from the race track. Many a horseman has tried to make a manageable hack or hunter out of a former race horse and has had to give up. Such horses have learned to gallop at top speed only, and to change all that is often impossible. Yet Major Tuttle performed the most intricate maneuvers, requiring the complete control and obedience of his mount, with nothing for a bridle and bit but a silken thread.

The great Exterminator was a true gentleman among horses. You could truthfully say of him that he never was guilty of stubbornness, meanness, or stupidity. He also imposed his ideas of behavior on others. Mars Cassidy, who was the starter at the New York tracks in earlier days, said that Exterminator was the best assistant starter he ever had. Not only by his perfect behavior did he set an example for the more unruly members of a field, but on more than one occasion he leaned over and pinned a bad actor into position.

Seabiscuit, that grand old campaigner, was an individualist with ideas of his own. He was as game as they come, but he saw no reason for doing more than necessary to win. Other horses ran their legs off when they were ten lengths in front, but not Seabiscuit. A head or even a nose was enough for him. Also he hated morning workouts.

The great Exterminator was one of the most intelligent horses of his day. It was said of him that he never did a stupid thing. He ran his own race, made his own pace, and went to a drive when he was ready. The jockey just went along for the ride.

"He was a lazy old fellow," said his exercise boy. "He would get out there on the track, mornings, and blow and puff as if working his very hardest. I would yell, 'Ah, you Biscuit,' and he would just cock his ear back and start puffing and carrying on as if he was doing his level best. We knew he wasn't, but we never did much about it because he seemed to know more about getting himself fit than anyone else."

Even on race days Seabiscuit was something of an actor. Many fine horses have such pride and arrogance that they intimidate their opposition the moment they step onto the track. Not so Seabiscuit. On his way to the post he walked wearily, with a low head and lackluster eye. It was almost as if he were trying to disarm his opponents with the idea that he was a poor old worn-out horse with barely strength to drag himself along. At the barrier the story was different—he had the speed of a sprinter and very few horses outbroke him.

On a farm in Pennsylvania lived a horse that had real personality and more cleverness than might be wished for. His name was Thoughtful, which was not entirely appropriate if it suggests unselfish devotion. If he had a child on his back he was consideration itself, going quietly and not making a false move, but with a grown person he was a different mount. Behind every bush and tree lurked some fearful thing and his shies at these imaginary terrors were really something. Many a rider walked back after starting out for a quiet hack on Thoughtful, for he always saw something particularly terrifying when he felt his rider careless and relaxed in the saddle. This was only when hacking, which he loathed. Hunting was his game and there was no nonsense here. Let him see hounds, and fifty yelling Indians could not turn him from the line. He was only fifteen and a half hands, but no fence could stop him when hounds were running.

On the farm he was never fenced in. This was not sentiment; no fence could hold him. Because he had a favorite spot to water, at a brook that ran through the farm, he would sail over a four-foot-six post and rail. To see if the grass in the next field was sweeter he would jump a five-foot fence, top of which was a strand of barbed wire, put there with the hope that it might discourage him. A good hunter could jump these obstacles if put at them, but not many would do it of their own accord.

A locked door was nothing to Thoughtful if there was grain behind it. After a number of combinations on the stable-door lock failed to stop him—no one could figure that out!—his owners resorted to a padlock. It was a nuisance to use, but at least it would stop this thief, who was already too roly-poly for his own good. But he was not to be so easily beaten. After trying, unsuccessfully, to get the door open, he walked away in apparent disgust. The next morning, when the stable was unlocked, there was Thoughtful, gorged with grain from the open feedbins. He had watched his chance and slipped in when the stable door was left open for a moment and hidden himself in an empty stall at the dark end of the stable. When the stable was locked for the night he opened the various bins and helped himself to his heart's content.

The men who have spent a lifetime with horses are the best judges of them and it is noted that these men think of their horses in almost the same way that they do of people. Jimmy Jones, of famed Calumet Farm, learned horses in a good school, for his father, Ben Jones, is one of the great trainers of all time. These two men know their horses so well that they could scarcely be closer to them if they could converse. Anything at all amiss with any of their many charges is noticed at once, and the horses clearly know this.

Armed was, in his prime, the greatest of the handicappers. His intense courage made him a favorite of Jimmy Jones. They had a game that they always played. If the bay gelding did not come to the stall door with a fierce show of teeth and whites of eyes in evidence, something was wrong. This was a routine they had built up between them. Jones always pretended to be frightened; later he gave Armed the expected carrot. If a visitor was present Jones always explained that all the Bull Leas bite, but this one was the worst of all. Armed seemed to take this all in, becoming fiercer by the minute. When the trainer finally opened the stall door and went in to feel the horse's legs, Armed stood quietly, looking a little like a six-year-old bandit that had been unmasked.

"They will have to rank him with the great of all time," said the trainer with a world of pride in his voice. "He's lost that old 'zing' and the things he did easily come hard now, but when he was at his best there wasn't anything around that could touch him."

Much has been written about Brown Jack, a great English Cup horse who probably had the most definite personality of any horse on record. Steve Donoghue, the noted jockey who always rode him, writes: "I find it hard to write of Brown Jack as if he were an ordinary horse, or even a horse at all. If you think of a perfect gentleman with a few strange and particular habits of his own, that was Brown Jack. He was the most delightfully mannered gentleman you could wish to meet. He was also the gamest, most intelligent and generous horse that ever looked through a bridle."

Brown Jack began as a chaser and was one of the best. When

his trainer noted the tremendous burst of speed he had between fences he decided to try him on the flat. He would have won at the first asking if his intense curiosity had not intervened. He had no difficulty in keeping up with the pace but was plainly bewildered by the fact that there were no jumps. He looked from left to right as if to say, "What kind of a race is this, anyway? When do we come to the jumps?" He must have finally figured it out, for the next time he went about his business and won by a head. From then on he won most of his races but rarely by as wide a margin as would have been possible. Racing was a game with him, a series of individual contests. As he came up to a horse he would run stride for stride with him, then put on pace and pull away to engage the next one. By the time the stretch was reached there was usually just one horse ahead of him. Lengthening his enormous stride he would pass and pull away. As he approached the finish line he would prick his ears and put in a little quick stride or two that Donoghue called a dance step, and gallop across the line, reveling in the applause that always greeted him.

Getting Brown Jack ready for the races was another matter, and not a simple one. On the racecourse he would give everything for the asking, but not so on the home training grounds. He saw no reason to run his heart out with no one to watch or applaud, so he went through the motions of galloping without getting up the speed of a plow horse. The home grounds were routine to him, and certainly the exercise boy in a sweater was no jockey, so why waste energy on such nonsense? Punishment was out of the question for such a grand performer, and he was the type that would resent punishment intensely, so the only thing to do was to humor him and try to make workouts important.

A van was driven into the stable yard, and with a great deal of bustle and excitement, Brown Jack and his companion Mail Fist were driven to a course some distance away. Their riders would appear in racing silks and the start was made just as in a race. Then Brown Jack would bear down and show what he really could do. But let Donoghue show up in a sweater and the big horse just plodded along at an easy gallop. He was like a child that always wants any occasion to be a party, not a makeshift thing.

Ascot was his favorite course and it was there that he did his best racing. Although he was the homespun type, far removed from the usual conception of the Thoroughbred, and Ascot was the aristocrat of meetings, things were done there on a scale he liked. He even seemed to know when the Ascot meeting was due, for in the week or two preceding it there was no trouble in getting him to really gallop in his workouts.

When he won the famed Alexandria Stakes for the sixth time at the age of ten, the usually staid English crowd went wild. This time there was more than polite hand clapping and cries of "Well done." Hats were thrown in the air and the cheering was deafening as Brown Jack bowed right and left on his way back past the stands. This was not only a horse, and a great one, but a personality—debonair, colorful, and courageous. A true gentleman.

TEMPERAMENT

The variety of temperament and disposition in horses, and its causes, is truly fascinating. There is as great a variation as in people, and merely grouping horses under the heading of "well-mannered" and "tough ones" is scarcely more accurate than dividing the human race into good people and bad people.

Some horses are so docile that they will obey instantly, with an almost nervous eagerness to anticipate your wishes. Some are intelligent enough to obey only when what they are asked seems reasonable and in line with their previous training. Others obey only grudgingly and if they sense any uncertainty will immediately take advantage of it. Bluffers at heart, they will instantly back down in the face of discipline.

There are a few horses that are naturally mean, treacherous, and thoroughly undependable, regardless of training. Such animals are worse than useless and should not be accepted, even as a gift.

Beyond and above these are the rebels, the high-spirited individualists who do not yield readily to discipline, and fight if force is used. This kind the English call high-couraged, and it is not a bad designation, for usually courage and a strong competitive spirit accompany such a disposition.

Since a specific example is always more interesting than a generalization, we might take the Bad Boy of all bad boys: Display. Fair Play, his sire, had plenty of fire and all of his offspring had their share, but Display had three or four helpings—maybe more.

Display was not mean or tricky. The chip was on his shoulder for all to see. He planted his feet solidly and dared anyone to force him to do anything he did not want to do. Running he liked; it was in his blood. But standing at the barrier and being hauled about by an assistant starter was not for him. He fought that from the start and became known as the worst post horse of his time.

Perhaps we should go to the days of the old West to find a true parallel for the renegades of the turf. Those two-gun men of bygone days, who went into combat with the zest of a man approaching a feast, would have understood Display and other horses who never conformed. They had courage and, most of all, a rebellious spirit. In a way it was very much the sort of spirit that built our country, for in the beginning it was the discontented and misfits who came to a savage land to look for a new life. Those who were content to conform stayed at home. As a result, Americans are still rebellious at heart and look askance at any law that limits their freedom.

Possibly the best picture ever given of Display was that by the noted Thoroughbred authority J. A. Estes at the time of the horse's death. It was a fitting epitaph for the "Iron Horse."

"One of the least forgettable recollections of my life is that of the first look I had at Display after they brought him back to the farm to enter stud. I had never seen him race but I knew his reputation. He had fought, savaged, bucked, kicked, and slammed on nearly every race track east of the Mississippi, and starting crews never heaved a more heartfelt sigh of relief than when he was sent back to the farm for good.

"I peeped between the boards of a high fence. It was a long paddock, and Display was patrolling its length. Up and down, back and forth, never stopping. There was no other horse in sight but there were, apparently, some horses over the hill and Display was straining for a sight of them.

"He wore a muzzle. On each of his forefeet was strapped a heavy chain. The chains hampered his actions and slowed him down but they could not still the restless energy, the unexampled liveliness within him. He was imperious and impatient of restraint.

"The fires burnt high in him. He should have lived with the wild horses of the prairie where he could have been boss. There the issue would have been settled quickly; he would have ruled or died. But civilization got him instead. Men laid hold of his bridle. 'All right,' said Display, 'you asked for it,' and he gave it to them. Finally he did what they asked but not because he had changed his mind.

"Now they had him on the farm. With fences and chains and padding on the walls of his stall . . . but the fire didn't burn out. It seethed and raged within him, and outside when the chance came.

"Maybe I remember wrong after all. But this is what I remember about Display. And I always loved the old hellion. He was like the hero of an old Greek tragedy, the pattern of his life tortured by an inner compulsion in conflict with the unalterable restraints of fate. He was beaten into the boundaries men prepared for him but his spirit never yielded an inch."

And this fiery rebel was at one time the leading money-winner in the world! Purses were small in those days and he had none of the larger two- and three-year-old stakes to help him, for he was a late-maturing horse, as were so many of the Fair Plays. Almost all of it was won in the handicap division, usually under top weight. He never started in a race without a pitched battle at the

Display—the rebel of all rebels. He never took a step backward from anyone.

start. How he could have won so often, after having dragged a couple of assistant starters all over the track for ten or fifteen minutes, is still a miracle. He was indeed an iron horse.

There is a world of difference between a mean, treacherous horse and a tough and even dangerous one. A horse like Display was, in a sense, absolutely trustworthy. You knew just what to expect. This was no gangster that hid in a dark corner and shot you in the back. He met you in the open, asked for no quarter and gave none. Perhaps he would have been different if he had not met compulsion at the starting barrier. Still, it would probably have come elsewhere. Such a violently independent spirit was not made for this world.

More than a century ago a slim, quiet-spoken man named James Rarey proved his claim that few horses are naturally vicious but are made so by man. Using hobbles he rendered horses helpless, and then by gently stroking and caressing them made killers into manageable mounts in a matter of hours. He created such an impression in Europe, where he exhibited his skill before royalty, that he was hailed as the greatest horseman of his day. He used neither whip nor spur and fully lived up to his motto: "A horseman should know neither fear nor anger."

Years ago when the cavalry was still an important adjunct to the army, it obtained a fine stallion for its remount service called Burning Blaze. He was a Thoroughbred of great quality and the remount was only able to get him because of his violent temper. He would bite, strike, and cow-kick most viciously, and it took two men with long lead shanks to safely take him out of his stall. As was the practice, the horse was put out at a ranch so cattlemen would breed to him, thus improving the stock of the area and making better horses available for the cavalry.

Elkridge—model of perfect disposition, and a flawless performer over the jumps. A true champion.

Several months later, when it was time to vaccinate him, the army veterinary of the area, Major Drum, and an assistant proceeded to the ranch where he was at stud. The rancher was not at home, but they found Burning Blaze in a corral. After instructing his assistant to arm himself and come to his aid if the horse got him down, the Major warily entered the corral. To his amazement the former demon approached, nuzzled him, and permitted himself to be vaccinated without trouble. It seems likely that someone early in the horse's career had changed a spirited horse into a dangerous rebel.

Sometimes a horse is called a "rogue" when he is only a rugged individualist with a mind of his own. Such a one was a great English horse named Santoi. He was in his day the best stayer in England, and the noted jockey Tod Sloan, who was the greatest rider of the time, stated that he was one of the two best horses he had ever ridden. This despite the fact that he all but made a fool of his rider.

At the peak of his career, under vigorous training, Santoi evidently decided he had done enough. From then on his sole idea was to circumvent those who tried to make him race. They got him to the post well enough, and around the course, but only on his own terms. He merely galloped leisurely behind the field. Everything was tried but Santoi had become cunning. He saw through all the subterfuges and none worked.

Finally the great Tod Sloan was sent for. He found that the horse went kindly for him in a workout, so he consented to try him in a race. They got to the post without difficulty, but when the starter's flag fell, there stood Santoi, watching the field dash away. In disgust Sloan turned the horse toward his stable. In that instant Santoi grabbed the bit and dashed after the field, a half furlong ahead. Sloan, realizing how futile such an effort was, tried to pull him down but without success. Suddenly he realized how freely the big horse was running and how rapidly they were gaining; he sat down and began driving. Instantly he felt the horse pull up. Quickly Sloan realized what he must do with this obstinate rebel.

He began sawing at the reins as if trying to pull up, and Santoi again took hold of the bit and bent to his work. From then on Sloan did everything he could to convince Santoi that he was running away with his rider. It took nerve to prevent Sloan from riding one of his famous slashing finishes, for it was very close as the finish line approached, but Santoi went across the line a head in front, with Sloan still sawing at the reins.

The cheering and applause evidently convinced Santoi that he had been outsmarted, for no one was ever able to make him extend himself again. He had done a lot in races over punishing distances—he felt it was enough, and man had better agree with him. Many have regretted that rebellion ran so high in such fine horses as Display and Santoi, but who knows if the stretch drive would have had that fierce tenacity if the blood had run cooler. A trainer once remarked, "I've made tough horses into quiet ones but they were never as good race horses afterwards. They were best when they were tough—the way they were meant to be."

They all have their qualities, even the toughest ones, but many of the greatest were without fault: Exterminator, whose behavior was as flawless as his performance; Hindoo, who was "like wax in the hands of his jockey"; Seabiscuit, who had a heart almost too big for his body; and Display, who never took a backward step for anybody.

CONFORMATION

In many ways beauty and good conformation are synonymous. Symmetry, balance, and rhythm are found alike in the works of Da Vinci and in Equipoise, in Man o' War and in the Winged Victory of Samothrace. An artist might look at any of these for hours and find nothing he would add and nothing that could be taken away. Each line and form has a function that relates to the whole and is in perfect harmony with the rest.

It has been said that the surest way to give a person true artistic appreciation is to surround him with fine art from earliest childhood. Thus his eye will become accustomed to perfection and he will reject trash through feeling rather than reasoning. Undoubtedly the same method would work in acquiring "an eye for a horse."

Since few people would have a chance to follow this idea it might be helpful to set down some of the commonly accepted marks of quality in a horse. The old saying that "a horse should fill the eye" is of questionable value. Obviously one person's eye is much more easily filled than another's. With experience you may find your taste changed considerably. The horse that filled your eye last year may, in the face of wider experience, be a mere mote.

An eye for a horse is not a gift, but something acquired by many years of intelligent observation and experience. Few have it. It goes beyond the mere observation of good points. Many years of experience have taught what each good point is apt to mean in performance and what each poor point will count for on the other side of the ledger. A novice may be full of praise or criticism the moment he sets eyes on a horse. An experienced trainer will step back and study a horse with absorbing intensity for ten minutes before he says a word. And remember, he can see more at a glance than most of us can in an hour.

He will step back a dozen paces so that he can see the horse as a whole, see his proportion and balance, before he is interested in any details. A good horse should have a deep shoulder. This calls for a big, well-developed chest. From the point of the shoulder to the withers the line should be sloping. A horse with an upright shoulder will have poor action galloping, lack the reaching stride of a stayer, and never be a good jumper. He should be deep through the heart—that is, the girth line—as this is a sign of stamina. A horse cannot be too deep through the heart, any more than a man can be too broad in the shoulders. All the best horses have been deep through the heart—our greatest ones very notably so.

He should be close-coupled and well ribbed up, with no slackness through the loins. If he is cut away too much where the body joins the hindquarters he is called light-waisted, and such a horse cannot carry weight or stand much work. The quarters should be full and muscular. A straight croup line is to be preferred, but a sloping one, or *goose rump*, is not necessarily a defect. Many good jumpers have been goose-rumped.

Since most of the propelling power comes from the quarters, the hind legs are very important. The hock should be as straight as possible and a *well let down hock*, one that is low-set, is considered very essential. In fact the lower both hock and knee are, the better. A *sickle hock*, which is the opposite of a straight hind leg, is a real defect and is rarely seen on a good horse. The muscle just above the hock, called the *gaskin*, should be very strong and well developed, for it is of utmost importance in galloping. There should be good bone below the knee and clean, pencil-like tendons. Most lameness in a horse comes in the foreleg below the knee, so soundness there is of the greatest importance. The pasterns should be long enough to be sloping and flexible. In a heavy-weight hunter the pasterns are shorter and more upright than in a race horse.

The forelegs should be straight. However, being *over at the knee* is often due to hard work and competition; consequently it cannot always be regarded as a defect in conformation. When the phrase *plenty of bone* is used, it refers to the cannon bone, and the measurement is taken between the knee and the pastern. Eight and a half to nine inches in circumference is desirable. In jumpers this is an especially important point.

The neck should be well set on, strong and arched. A *ewe neck*, which is thin and with the top line concave, is an eyesore as well as a weakness. Experienced horsemen have maintained that a horse tires first in the neck, so a strong, flexible neck of good length is very necessary to a good horse.

The head should be on the small side in a well-bred horse, and there should be a feeling of leanness, with the bone structure, muscles, and veins sharply defined, especially in a race horse. Too much fleshiness in the head suggests lack of blood and quality. The eyes should be large and prominent, clear and alert. Horsemen will often spend more time studying the head, and particularly the eyes, than any other part. Often the fire and courage a horse has is clearly written there.

The ears should be active and constantly moving, as this shows mental alertness. There have been many fine horses with *lop ears*,

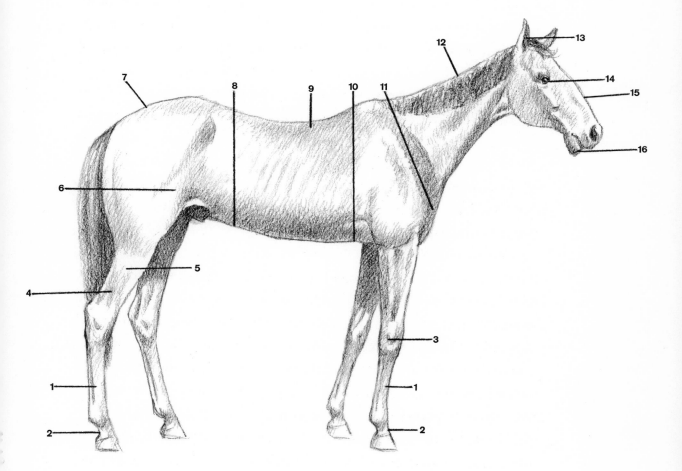

Exaggerated sketch of a horse of bad conformation

1. Light bone   2. Short, straight pasterns   3. Over at knee   4. Sickle hock
5. Weak gaskins   6. Weak quarters   7. Goose rump   8. Light waist
9. Sway-back   10. Lack of depth through girth   11. Straight shoulder
12. Ewe neck   13. Lop ears   14. Pig eye   15. Roman nose   16. Slack lip

so it is wise not to be too critical on this point. However, small well-set ears add much to the appearance of keenness in a horse.

A good horse should be wide between the eyes, for this is where the brain is located. Many horsemen will not take a horse as a gift if he is narrow between the eyes. Seen from the side the line of the nose and head should be quite straight. A curved, or Roman nose means that horse has a will of his own and may be a handful. Man o' War, and most of his offspring, had a trace of Roman nose—and also a trace of what went with it.

The head should taper to a certain fineness at the muzzle; the nostrils should be full and flaring, as it is only through them that a horse can breath. In short, the head should show the breeding and quality in a horse—when it is there even the novice is aware of it. Honesty and courage are written as clearly in a horse's head as in a man's face.

There is usually considerable difference in the conformation of a sprinter and a stayer. The sprinter is usually heavier muscled and blockier than a stayer. Many of the great sprinters have been gigantic horses, muscled like weight-lifters. By their appearance you would think they had the power to run all day, but a slimmer build with long muscles is usually the mark of the stayer.

Size is of no consideration in judging the quality of a horse. If he gains in power without becoming clumsy a large horse has an advantage, although some horsemen are prejudiced against large horses. James Rowe, a great trainer, felt so strongly about it that he would never admit that Man o' War was a great horse, always referring to him as "that big lobster." Perhaps the fact that the big red horse mowed down the best Rowe could send against him had much to do with his prejudice.

"A good horse is never a bad color" is an old saying around the

Kelso, one of the greatest stayers, performed the unprecedented feat of winning the two-mile Jockey Club Gold Cup for three successive years. Here is the conformation usually seen in a true stayer: short-coupled with well let down hocks and knees, which altogether gives longer stride.

In this fine mare, Bewitch, almost perfect conformation can be seen.

tracks. There are certain prejudices about color, nevertheless. Horsemen do not like a washed-out chestnut or a light bay. Whatever his color they like it to be a dark shade. As a Negro groom put it, "Man or hoss, if he's black I like to see him good an' black. They're better that way."

A dark bay with black points and the black running well above the knee and hock is looked on with great favor. Too much white is frowned on—even a white stocking, since it means a light-colored hoof, which hasn't the toughness of a dark hoof. In the old English hunting days the prejudice against too much white went very deep, as the old rhyme suggests:

> *Four white feet and a white nose,*
> *Cut off his head and give him to the crows.*

Gallant old Jolly Roger, one of the greatest steeplechasers, disproved the rhyme for all time, for he was white to the knees and hocks and half his face was white.

Newcomers to the turf are sometimes surprised to see a horse listed as brown that to their eyes is black. This was true in the case of War Admiral, whose coat was black except under strong sunlight when warm color showed in the flanks and the muzzle. The color of a horse is determined by the hair on his muzzle, which never changes. Gray horses become lighter as they grow older and some that are almost black in their youth end up almost white with age. All horses that range from deep iron-gray to pure white are officially listed as gray.

A horse in good condition has a *bloom*, or sheen, to his coat that is not present when he is stale or unfit. Hirsch Jacobs, who has led the trainers' list many years with claiming horses and "cripples," was asked for the secret of his success. He said he merely watched his horses carefully and ran them when he thought they were fit. "When a horse looks good he feels good," he said, "and when he feels good he runs good."

In all the charts and graphs, the most important quality of a horse is not touched upon. No matter how perfect the conformation, how fine the breeding, it is wasted if the horse hasn't "plenty of heart." That combination of courage, fire, and pride is the motor and without it nothing works. Perhaps the phrase might even be taken literally, for it was found after his death that the great, unbeaten Eclipse had a heart that weighed fourteen pounds—twice that of the average horse.

A word of warning might not be amiss. "A little knowledge is a dangerous thing." There are too many self-appointed critics of horseflesh who learned the difference between a hock and a pastern only yesterday. Some of them haven't got it straight yet, but their critical comments are hampered not a whit by this. You must see horses a long time before any but the most obvious defects are visible to you. The true horseman sees much and says little. We can emulate him to some degree if knowing little, we say little.

TRAINING

Although a young horse's life is made up mostly of playing, eating, and sleeping, there must be a little training too. He should be taught to be obedient when the blacksmith is called in, and raise each foot on command. Until he is old enough for shoes, his feet must be trimmed every five or six weeks. Good blacksmiths are hard to find and they have little patience with difficult horses, so it is wise to teach the youngster manners as early as possible. If he learns to follow willingly when led, even into a trailer or horse van, that is so much to the good. It can save a lot of time and trouble in the future.

When leading a horse do not pull straight forward if he plants his feet and refuses to budge. Turn him to the right, then the left, and get him moving; then you can go in the direction you originally intended. Never let it be a tug of war. That is a contest you can never win, and one such battle can stay in his mind forever. A horse has a long memory.

If handled with intelligence he should seldom have a chance to be successful in disobedience. When he is rebellious about something, unless it is imperative it might be better not to present it at that time. On another day his mood may be different and the thing he resented may not seem objectionable. He is a reasoning animal with the mentality, approximately, of a six-year-old boy. If thought of in this way his training is a simpler matter.

Patience is of utmost importance. A horse reluctant to enter a new stable or van must be given all the time in the world. He simply cannot be forced. If it is attempted he may well be a *bad loader* the rest of his life. The surest way to dispel his distrust of a strange stall is to let him see everything and feel he has his own choice. Even the offer of grain will not help if he feels the slightest suggestion of force. If he is held on a long shank, and allowed to look around at everything and make up his mind there is nothing to be feared, he will walk in of his own accord. It may take time but if patience is used, the problem is solved for good.

The procedure for breaking horses varies according to the type and to the area in which it is going to be used. The method employed with Thoroughbreds destined for the racecourse is so well and carefully planned that it might serve as a model. Here the greatest consideration is given the individual and nothing is too much trouble. The same methods should work well with other breeds.

Breaking is hardly the proper term, for the process is so gradual that often the yearlings do not realize what is happening. Grooms make a practice of putting an arm over the youngster's back and resting a little weight on it so that a saddle and rider will not seem so strange when the time comes. A saddle is usually put on from time to time with the girth loose. As this becomes routine the girth is tightened a little each time. By the time a light boy mounts him in the stall for the first time, the yearling takes it without much fuss. From this to walking and jogging with a rider up is but another small step. Since no speed is used at first, response to reins is automatic, for there is no reason for refusal. The schooling that produces the well-mannered youngster ready for races is now just a matter of time, and more patience.

Probably the TV Westerns are responsible for more bad riding and spoiling of horses than any other influence. The youngster brought up on this fare thinks that a horseman never goes at any pace but a full gallop and that he should be broken into this pace from a standstill. A horse so handled will become absolutely worthless as a pleasant hack or a safe mount for youngsters. Even the race horse, whose life is speed and more speed, is taught to walk, jog, and go at a slow canter until asked for real pace.

A car that goes into high when you try to put it in low is certainly a hazard. Just so with a horse that takes the bit and uses his own idea of pace; or the youngster who completely ignores parental advice. Obedience and response are as important with a young horse as with a young child—perhaps more so, for he is stronger and harder to discipline.

The young Thoroughbreds that are meant for the race track are usually broken in the fall, when they are eighteen to twenty months old and approaching their full growth. Although not yet mature, they weigh between eight and nine hundred pounds and are within an inch or two of their full height. Although breaking is usually a simple matter, because of preliminary training, there are occasional rebels. Man o' War fought like a tiger when first mounted and threw his rider again and again. When he finally realized what was expected of him he became manageable, although he was never a horse you could be careless with.

Such battles are to be avoided if possible, for violent action of this sort puts great strain on muscles and ligaments not fully developed and toughened. All efforts are made to avoid any nervousness and fear. For this reason they are handled in groups so they gain confidence from their companions. Horses are very gregarious and are only happy when others are near-by. When

Fire as well as a good disposition can often be found in a horse that has had good training.

out at pasture they will always be together in a compact group, regardless of how green the grass may be in other parts of the paddock.

After plenty of time at the slower paces so they are well *legged up*, they may be *breezed* for a furlong or two. This calls for close to top speed and is usually done in pairs. Thus the trainer begins to get an idea of what he has in his stable. The more promising ones are made eligible for important two-year-old stakes. Of course the trainer takes into consideration that some of the youngsters are precocious and have their speed early, while some of their slower-developing fellows may prove to be better horses. He relies not only on his experience in sizing up a horse, but also on the breeding pattern of the youngsters. He knows the ones with sprinting blood in their pedigrees can be counted on to show their speed earlier than those of staying lines, but they will almost certainly have a shorter tether. But even more than this, he looks for those that show a strong competitive spirit. Without that, looks, conformation, and even speed are nothing.

At their winter training grounds the two-year-olds come out in *sets* of from four or five to a dozen, with a stable pony in front to set an example of quiet behavior. There is no need to ask if these are two-year-olds; their quick, nervous action tells the story. A horse gallops past and they are all over the track. They expect the worst and if it doesn't happen some trifle will serve the purpose. Down the stretch comes the drum roll of galloping hoofs, an exciting sound for man or beast, and the two-year-olds scatter in all directions. You can scarcely blame them, but they have to learn about the excitement of the race track early. It will be their life for the next few years, maybe longer if there are any really good ones here.

Often after one of these alarms there is an exercise boy in the dirt and a loose horse galloping up the track. Everything stops until the runaway is caught and examined for possible cuts and bruises—no one thinks of looking for the boy. Around the track the horse always comes first. When the boy appears, dusty and sheepish, he is advised to buy a pot of glue for his pants.

As a set gallops along one of the boys will often begin singing in time to the pace and the others join in. The horses seem to enjoy this and even cock back an ear to hear it. Almost all riders talk, croon, or sing to their horses and it has a quieting effect on them. One of the top riders comes along on a big skittish colt that puts in a buck and kick every few strides. "You big bum," he croons. "Go along, you big bum." Soon the colt settles down to a long, swinging gallop, apparently enjoying the rhythmic, affectionate abuse directed at him.

The riders rarely lose their tempers with the horses and are surprisingly patient with even the flightiest of the two-year-olds. A little chestnut filly shies suddenly and bolts across the track. It looks for a minute as if she might crash into the rail in a bad spill, but her rider straightens her out just in time. He quiets her with voice and hand, merely observing, "All fillies are dillies." The other boys all agree with this bit of worldly cynicism.

When the youngsters have learned to gallop together smoothly without swerving and have been breezed a few times, they are introduced to the starting gate. This is a rather terrifying object to a young horse, and the first few times he may only be brought down to stand beside it. Finally he is led into one of the stalls, but the doors are kept open so he can go on through if he becomes nervous. When he has become accustomed to the gate and will stand quietly, the next step is taken. The gates are closed and the bar is placed behind him as in a racing start. He is kept in the locked stalls for a few minutes to adjust to that confinement, then the gates are opened quietly and he is walked out. All this is done slowly and patiently so that he will finally learn to stand quietly and wait for the doors to fly open as the starter's bell sends the horses on their way. Patience at this time can make the difference between a "good post horse" and a "bad actor."

After weeks of training at slower paces, the youngster is far enough along to be asked for speed. The schedule will now usually call for a breeze every third day, with slow gallops in between. Breezes vary in pace but are always pretty close to racing speed. As the spring racing season draws near, the breezes are lengthened until the youngsters are doing half miles within a few seconds of their top effort. The early races will be at five furlongs and they are now in condition for such a distance.

The race horse has often finished his day's work before many of us have started ours, as most workouts take place as soon as it is daylight. By ten o'clock he is back at the stable, walking in a circle under a *cooler*, or thin blanket. Each horse has his own bucket, set on a bench near the walking ring, and is allowed to stop for a sip of water every few minutes. Within half an hour he will ignore his bucket and be dry under the sheet. He is now *cooled out* and ready to be put back in his stall for the rest of the day.

Soon will come a day when he will be led out in the afternoon and taken to the saddling enclosure. There will be a jockey in bright silks to be tossed into the saddle as the bugle blows "Boots and Saddles." He is on his way.

THE MEASURE OF GREATNESS

The qualifications of greatness in a horse have undergone considerable change in the last century. In the days of Boston and his great son Lexington, stamina was the primary requisite, as indeed it had to be in those days of four-mile heats. It seems more than likely that the strain of racing three four-mile heats in an afternoon put too great a premium on stamina at the sacrifice of speed, for as races were shortened the names of those great progenitors Boston and Lexington appeared less and less frequently in the pedigrees of the top racers. Today that famous line which once dominated the American turf is dead.

Coming down to the 1880's we have a galaxy of famous names: Hindoo, Hanover, Bramble, and Himyar. Hindoo is generally accepted as the greatest of these. How to evaluate a horse like Hindoo in relation to the best horses of our own time is a problem. Those who saw him are no longer with us, and even if they were, the mere memory of a great horse may take on an added glory with the passing years. He dominated his rivals, but again we have no way to judge the opposition. The only measure left us is the most uncertain one of comparative time.

It is well known that the tracks have been made faster with the passing years, but exactly to what degree is hard to estimate. Our track equipment is better and more efficient; more money is spent on the right mixture of soil and sand to provide cushion and drainage. Last but not least, the publicity that attends new track records has not gone unnoticed and everything is done to insure fast time. A track like Belmont, with the tradition of the finest racing in America, has never gone to extremes in this matter. Safety for the horses has always taken precedence over track records, and the same is true of Saratoga. Churchill Downs is faster now than in the old days, perhaps by as much as several seconds to the mile; but scarcely enough to span the gap between the time of Hindoo's day and ours. As a three-year-old, carrying 105 pounds, Hindoo ran a mile and a half in 2:40. The Belmont Stakes for three-year-olds is at the same distance and was run by Count Fleet under 126 pounds in 2:28⅕. Since horsemen figure one-fifth of a second to a length, the time difference between Hindoo and Count Fleet would equal fifty-nine lengths. The differential in weight carried would add to this unbelievable figure. Handicappers estimate two pounds to a length, thus twenty-one pounds would make ten and a half lengths. According to figures then, Count Fleet would be almost seventy lengths in front of that hero of the eighties. This no horseman in his right mind would believe. But still, that vast gap cannot be explained by the differences in the tracks. The only explanation is that "improvement of the breed" is not merely a phrase, but a definite, tangible thing. If today's track star can run a mile twenty seconds faster than the athlete of the eighties, why is it not logical to assume that the Thoroughbred has improved to a comparable extent?

In 1904 Sysonby came on the scene, hailed by some old-time horsemen as the superior of Man o' War. Like Man o' War he was beaten but once. Since as two-year-olds their time at five and a half furlongs was almost identical, it is fair to assume the tracks and track conditions were about on a par. But here the similarity ends. Sysonby carried 107 pounds in the Metropolitan Handicap in 1:41⅖. Man o' War ran the same distance under 118 pounds in 1:35⅘. The track variant might explain a little of this great difference but not all of it. This is clear when we go to the longer distances. At Saratoga, Sysonby, under 119 pounds, ran a mile and a quarter in 2:07. On the same track Man o' War ran the same distance in 2:01⅘ carrying 129 pounds. Sysonby's best time at a mile and a half was 2:33⅕. Man o' War's was 2:28⅘.

Another that old-time horsemen said was greater than our best of today was the unbeaten Colin. At six furlongs his time and Man o' War's were identical. This must indicate that track conditions were very similar for both horses. Yet at the longer routes the story is very different. Colin's time for the Withers was 1:41. Man o' War's time for the mile was a full five seconds faster. At a mile and a quarter the story was almost the same. If, as their times indicate, the two horses would be nose and nose for six furlongs but Man o' War would lead by twenty-five lengths at the mile, a possible explanation comes up. Could it be possible that Colin was a sprinter that could not carry his speed over a distance? The evidence seems to say so.

This is the one kind of comparison that can be made, and the only one that has any validity. That it is far from accurate is admitted, but since the margin of difference in performances of the two eras is so very great, even inaccuracies could scarcely affect the conclusions. This is not to belittle the horses of earlier days but to try to draw a true comparison. If there is any truth in the maxim "breed the best to the best," it means that with time there will be an improvement in quality and ability. Of course there is always the exception. From somewhere comes a Babe Ruth, a Man o' War. The mold is broken and there may never be another. This is the peak. There can't be much improvement on perfection.

MAN O' WAR

"This is the mostest hoss," proclaimed Will Harbut, Man o' War's Negro groom, when he showed his charge to the thousands who came to see the great horse at Faraway Farm in Kentucky. Many have echoed the sentiment. Year after year we have horses that seem likely to threaten his supremacy, but as time goes on he still stands alone.

He was by Fair Play, one of our greatest sires, although decried by some because of his fiery temperament. High-headed (the mark of all his tribe), golden-coated Fair Play was one of the most beautiful horses to appear on the American turf. Mahubah, dam of Man o' War, was by the imported Rock Sand, a great brood-mare sire. Man o' War was foaled in 1917 at the Nursery Stud of Major August Belmont, Jr. Because he was going off to the war, Major Belmont decided to sell his yearlings. At first he intended to hold out Man o' War—doubtless he saw something unusual in the leggy red colt—but he finally included him in the Saratoga sale of August 17, 1918. Samuel D. Riddle bought the chestnut colt for $5,000, the greatest bargain in turf history. He bought a number of others and later remarked, "I paid $28,000 for eleven yearlings. Ten were blanks but the eleventh was Man o' War."

The big red colt first attracted attention when he was being broken, for he fought like a tiger and threw his rider time and again. It was only when he learned what was wanted that he became tractable, but always under saddle he was full of excitement. Running was in his blood and he gloried in speed. He sprang into the lead at once in his first start and opened more and more until he came roaring to the finish all by himself. From then on he was a marked horse, for that surge of power and fire of competition only the good ones have, and they not always.

His next start was in a stake, the Keene Memorial, and those who opposed him were of higher class. He had to come from behind, as he was off to a slow start, but once he got under full sail it was all over. He won by three lengths, easily beating On Watch, a highly rated colt. When he went to the post for the Youthful Stakes he was carrying 120 pounds, giving twelve pounds to On Watch and more to the others. He won by two and a half lengths under a pull. For his next start he was given 130 pounds! Most horses never carry such weight until they are four, yet Man o' War carried 130 pounds seven times as a two-year-old. In the Tremont, under that weight, only two colts could be found to oppose him and he led from start to finish.

Moving to Saratoga the big red colt was again under 130 pounds in the United Hotel Stakes, and he easily beat Upset, the only horse to ever finish in front of him. In the Sanford Stakes, carrying 130 pounds to Upset's 115, he got the worst of the start, and was pocketed in the stretch. When he got free it was too late. Most people blamed his jockey, Johnny Loftus, who never again got the mount on him, for poor judgment in trying to get through on the inside—there was no room. He was never beaten again and fully deserved to retire unbeaten, as later events proved.

The Grand Union Hotel Stakes gave the big red colt his revenge. Here he gave Upset five pounds and beat him decisively. The Hopeful was won by four lengths with Upset unplaced. In the Futurity he met all the top two-year-olds and again won as

Man o' War: "He was as near living flame as horses ever get." *Joe Palmer*

he pleased. A close analysis of the races and weights indicates that Man o' War was fifteen to twenty pounds better than any two-year-old of his year. He could carry that much more weight and still beat them.

The only hope trainers of other stables had for 1920 was that the big red colt should prove short of stamina, as had so many phenomenally fast two-year-olds. On his bloodlines he should run as far as horses go, but he might not run to his breeding. When the answer came in the Preakness they knew they would all be running for second money that year.

Mr. Riddle felt, as have many horsemen, that the first of May was too early to ask a three-year-old to go a mile and a quarter. Not until War Admiral did he send any of his colts to the Derby. That race in 1920 resolved itself into a duel between Paul Jones and Upset, the former winning by a head. Man o' War had no preliminary races to bring him up to the Preakness, so he was coming to this race off of workouts alone against seasoned horses. In addition he was giving weight to his field, for in those days these races were not at level weights as is the case today. It was evident from the start that several riders had instructions to take the big horse by the head and run him into the ground. The only difficulty with this strategy was they could not get to him. He won by a length and a half under a strong pull, Upset finishing second.

His first appearance in New York that year brought out record crowds. Sometimes a champion is so much the workmanlike performer that he lacks color, but this horse was made for the spotlight. His high-headed surging speed, that seemed limitless and that he wanted to use to the utmost, stirred the imagination. The power of that unbelievable stride, known to be the longest ever

Man o' War was one of the most majestic stallions of all time. He had greatness and he knew it.

seen on the track, also quickened the pulse. He was a star of the first magnitude, and on his way to becoming a national hero.

In the Withers he did not disappoint the crowds. His odds were so short, one to seven, that it was apparent that the race was all but conceded. The crowd did not come to bet but to see a flashing, high-headed horse run, and they saw all of that. Only two opposed him, and they offered no opposition. He broke in front and merely galloped to his field in new track-record time.

What the other trainers thought of him by this time can be judged by the fact that only one horse opposed him in the historic Belmont Stakes. Again he won, but this time by twenty lengths, and again a record was set. In the Stuyvesant Handicap he shouldered 135 pounds against 103 on the only other starter and won by eight lengths. Then came the Dwyer and this was a different story.

The veteran trainer Rowe had been so incensed by the defeat of the colts in his stable that he had called Man o' War "that big lobster." He had John P. Grier, a fine horse, ready for the race of his life on the day of the Dwyer. Getting eighteen pounds from Man o' War, Rowe felt this was Grier's day. Coming out of the chute on the far side of the track the horses were locked in such a head-and-head battle that the smaller Grier, on the outside, was completely hidden, and the crowd thought he had been left at the post. Then, momentarily, Grier got his head in front and the excitement grew intense as they realized that at last the big horse had found someone to run with him. Grier held his own to the head of the stretch and then fell back. Man o' War came to the wire in front by a length and a half, again breaking a track record.

From then on the big red horse met no opposition worthy of

the name. In the Miller Stakes the famous jockey Earl Sande rode him for the first time and said later that he "let him run for a furlong. It was like being on a runaway locomotive." The Lawrence Realization looked as if it would be a "walkover" until Mr. Riddle persuaded Walter Jeffords to enter his horse Hoodwink, on the promise that Man o' War would not make a show of him. The rider was instructed to let Hoodwink stay within a reasonable distance but this he could not do. The big horse took the bit and won by an estimated hundred lengths. Even though Belmont is much faster now, the record he set that day stood for thirty years. He won the Jockey Club Stakes at a mile and a half by fifteen lengths and set a record that held until his son War Admiral shaved a fifth of a second from it seventeen years later! What this horse could have done if there was anyone to run with him is hard to imagine.

Mr. Riddle always considered the Potomac Handicap Man o' War's finest race and many horsemen agree with him. Here he shouldered 138 pounds, a weight unheard of for a three-year-old, giving twenty-four pounds to Paul Jones, the Derby winner, and much more to the rest of the field. He again made his own pace and won, unextended, in new track-record time. Behind him also was Wildair, good enough to win the Metropolitan, but a thirty-pound concession did not help on this occasion. Nowadays if a top handicap horse is asked to give his rivals as much as ten pounds he often is withdrawn from the race.

Man o' War's last race was a match with Sir Barton. Seventy-five thousand dollars and a magnificent gold cup were offered by Kenilworth Park in Canada to the winner. In morning workouts the big red horse showed such speed that the clockers could not believe their watches. Unfortunately Sir Barton was not in his best form and the race proved no contest at all. Man o' War finished by himself and yet broke the track record by more than six seconds.

A really great horse must be one with no weakness. He should have the speed of a sprinter and the heart of a stayer. He must be able to carry weight and to make the pace or come from behind with equal facility. And most important of all he must be consistent. There must be no races that need excuses or explanation. The more one studies the record the more the conviction grows that this big red horse was a phenomenon whose like may not be seen again.

FAMOUS HORSES

All countries have had outstanding horses, and to try to evaluate them all would be an impossible task; it would seem best to limit the list to America and even to recent decades. The four-mile races of yesterday differ so much from racing today that it is impossible to compare horses of the two eras. Stamina was all-important, and speed as we know it was almost nonexistent, judging by time. Also, tracks were so much slower, even at the turn of the century, that any comparison is greatly to the disadvantage of the turf heroes of those far-off days, so it is better to keep to a period when tracks are comparable and distances similar.

In American racing all comparisons begin and end with the flaming chestnut horse that so caught the eye of horsemen and public that he became the measuring rod for all time. Those "as good as Man o' War" and those "better than Man o' War" have since fallen by the wayside. The Whirlaways and the Johnstowns, even the Citations and the Noors, have come and gone and now the ultimate praise is "the best since Man o' War." The phrase-makers of the turf world have reconsidered and reappraised: race horses are no longer "as good" and possibly never again "better."

Of the same era as Man o' War was the great Cup horse Exterminator. He was a true stayer in every sense of the word and, like Man o' War, without flaw. He could win at six furlongs or at two miles and always under top weight. He ran a hundred races and won fifty of them. It was only the weight he was forced to concede to his rivals that defeated him. "Old

Bones," as he was affectionately called, was the most popular horse of his day. He was a perfect gentleman at all times and the best post horse ever seen on the track. Being a gelding and therefore useless for breeding, he was campaigned long and strenuously. At last it was clear that age had taken its toll and he was running on his courage alone. Retired to the farm, he was given a small Shetland pony for a companion and they became inseparable. Many years later Exterminator was paraded up the stretch at Pimlico. The roar of applause that greeted him was heart-warming. He had been away a long time, but they still remembered him.

Equipoise must always rank as one of the truly great ones. As his name might indicate, he was the perfectly balanced horse. Here were rhythm and harmony, the very epitome of the Thoroughbred. He was a champion with the true qualifications: the speed of a sprinter and the bottom of a stayer. That is the horseman's ideal, and seldom found. So many horses with a high turn of speed have a short tether; so many stayers lack real speed. Equipoise had everything.

All through his career he was plagued by a bad foot. It all but canceled out a three-year-old campaign that promised to be brilliant, and most of his races were in the handicap division. In all he ran fifty-one races and won twenty-nine, being unplaced but eight times, and always under top weight. The noted turf writer Salvator wrote of him, "Here is a living harmony in horseflesh; an embodiment of rhythm and modulation, of point and counterpoint, that sang to the eye and made music in the heart."

The golden-coated Discovery was a late-developing horse, so he also had to do most of his winning in the handicap division,

Equipoise, the beloved "Chocolate Soldier"—perfection in conformation, disposition, and performance

where he earned the reputation of being one of the greatest weight carriers in our turf history. Son of tough Display, he inherited his sire's ruggedness and power, but fortunately not his temperament.

As was the case with that other great weight carrier, Exterminator, Discovery was rarely beaten except by the handicapper. He won under 139 pounds, conceding as much as twenty-two pounds to his field. Some stables with top horses have announced that their horses will not start if more than 130 pounds is allotted them. Yet this doughty warrior attempted the impossible by shouldering 143 pounds!

At stud he was proved to be a great brood-mare sire, so much so that when his proud owner was asked his formula for breeding a top horse, he said, "Just breed any sire to a Discovery mare." Though said in jest, there is plenty of truth in the remark. It was just the way he had bred the great Native Dancer.

Seabiscuit also did not reach his full stature until late in his career. There was one occasion when he could have been claimed for six thousand dollars! Yet he ended up as the greatest money winner in the world at his prime. It took six years and eighty-nine races to accomplish it, a campaign so rugged as to be almost unheard of.

He was a bay horse, very compact, and notably deep through the heart, as was only fitting, for he was one of the gamest of horses. Time after time he stood a grueling head-and-head drive the length of the stretch and usually had that little extra to get his dark head in front at the wire. Speed and stamina he had in abundance, but courage was his stock in trade. He had that to the hilt.

When a horse wins the Triple Crown, which includes the

Derby, the Preakness, and the Belmont, there is little doubt of his quality. There have been lucky winners in some of these races, but a horse needs more than luck to win all three. This a small dark colt by Man o' War accomplished in 1937. In winning the Belmont, the testing distance of a mile and a half that separates the men from the boys, or more accurately, the sprinters from the stayers, he broke the track record set by his famous sire so many years before. And it *was* many years before, for War Admiral was "an old man's son," from one of the last crops of foals. Completely unlike his sire in appearance, he was most like him in performance: impetuous and impatient at the barrier, pouring speed on speed to run his opposition into the ground from the start. He was headed for the heights but his eagerness at the start of the Belmont caused near disaster. He stumbled and in recovering sheared off a quarter of the heel of a forefoot. Although the injury was serious enough to sidetrack him for months, he finished by himself, fighting for his head all through the stretch as his great red sire had done before him. He ran many brilliant races when he returned to the track, but many horsemen believed he was never quite the same horse that he was in the Belmont. Often a horse fully recovered from an injury has lost a little of that dash—horsemen call it *zing*—that made everything so effortless. It comes only once.

Whirlaway of the one-eyed blinker and the flowing tail was to be the next Triple Crown winner. He was a sensational horse to watch, for he liked to drop far off the pace and then make a stretch run that was unbelievable. Often he was so far back at the far turn that his case seemed hopeless. Then he moved into high and the field in front came back to him. The few times he

Most horsemen consider Count Fleet one of the most brilliant horses in racing history.

was beaten were due to bearing out and going so wide on the turn that he lost a dozen lengths. A one-eyed blinker corrected this habit and then he was rarely beaten.

Although the Triple Crown is the most difficult achievement in racing, there were three brilliant performers who accomplished this feat in a short span of time. Count Fleet was a dark bay colt, nervous and high-strung, and not too prepossessing in conformation. He had such a high turn of speed that many horsemen thought he might merely be a sprinter. He liked to go to the front at once. Such a horse is always under suspicion until he proves he can go a distance. As a two-year-old he did not have to go beyond sprint distances, but at three he answered the question. In the Belmont Stakes he ran the mile and a half in new record time, winning as he pleased. An injury in the race terminated his career. As a three-year-old he was unbeaten, in fact he was never even brought to a drive. He was one of the great ones; just how great we will never know.

It is rare that an owner has the temerity to race a filly against the colts, for even with the weight allowance given a filly she is rarely a match for the sturdier males. The lone filly to win the Derby was Regret, but in later years we have had several fillies that could not only dominate their own division but also hold their own against the colts. The first of these was Calumet Farm's Twilight Tear. Next came the War Admiral filly Busher, whom many horsemen consider the best to have appeared in this country. She beat the colts more than once and even took the measure of the mighty Armed in the Washington Park Handicap, breaking the track record in doing so. Surprisingly, she was feminine in appearance, with a very fine head, for most of the fillies that are up to such rugged competition are amazons.

Stymie was truly the poor boy who made good. Starting in the cheapest claimers, he became the leading money winner of the world in his day.

Armed is generally considered the greatest gelding to appear on the track since Exterminator. He was a very versatile horse, for he was as dangerous at sprint distances as at longer routes. A tough, hardy campaigner, he ran eighty-one races in all and ended by taking from Seabiscuit the title of the world's greatest money winner.

Stymie, a high-headed chestnut horse, showed none of the attributes of a top horse in his first two years of racing. Running in even the cheapest of claimers, he seldom won. In his earliest days on the track he could have been claimed for fifteen hundred dollars, yet he ended up the winner of almost a million dollars. To have earned this in the toughest of competition, the handicap division, he had to be something special—and he was. Not since Whirlaway had there been such a stretch runner. Always last during the early part of a race, often by as much as twenty lengths, it did not seem possible that he could make up the ground. But when he hit the far turn his head came up a notch, and then he came like a ship under full sail and the opposition melted away. Usually that drive so annihilated his field that he would come striding to the wire all by himself. Always the crowd felt that they had seen the impossible, and the applause was tremendous.

He was the most popular horse of his day. The fact that it was the rags-to-riches story, with embellishments, did not hurt a bit. Added to that was the fact that he had a high-headed, regal dignity. He walked like a king.

Stymie had a right to be a good horse. The quality was slow in showing but it came from the best. Both his sire and dam were out of Man o' War mares.

Gallorette was a powerful mare who found the confines of

Citation was one of the truly great. At his peak nothing could touch him.

Tom Fool was one of the very best—fast, game, and consistent.

races for her sex too limited. She stepped out of her division and ended up by beating many of the best of the handicap horses. Big, rugged, and durable, she raced for three full seasons, running seventy-two times and ending up the biggest money winner of her sex.

Max Hirsh, the veteran horseman, who has trained so many fine horses, rates Assault as the best of them all. Although a rather small horse, he was a tremendous weight carrier, winning under 135 pounds. At three he joined the select circle of Triple Crown winners. Retired to stud after a most successful career, he seemed certain to be a successful sire also, but unfortunately he proved sterile.

Bull Lea, the most successful stallion in the history of the American turf, sired many fine performers, but in Citation he got one of the greatest of all time. Citation won the Triple Crown with such remarkable ease that most horsemen felt he was the best since Man o' War; some even proclaimed him better than that great horse. Until he suffered an injury at the end of his three-year-old campaign there was nothing around that could compare with him. His trainer, Jimmy Jones, feels that he was never quite the same horse after his injury, even though he ran some fine races later in California. His total earnings were $1,085,760. He was the first horse in the world to earn a million dollars.

Noor, a tall, leggy Irish-bred horse, gained fame for his great duels with Citation. Like all Irish horses he was bred with an eye to stamina, and he was a true stayer. One of his greatest races was in the mile-and-three-quarters San Juan Capistrano. He and Citation began their drive on the far turn and were head and head all through the long stretch. At the finish it was Noor by a nose

The big gray, Native Dancer, was beaten only once in his career.

in a new world record. So close was the competition that almost every time these two met the result was a new record.

Tom Fool was one of the handsomest horses of his day and also one of the very best, reaching his peak at four. It was then that he performed the all-but-impossible feat of capturing the Handicap Triple Crown. This consists of the three top handicaps, the Metropolitan, the Suburban, and the Brooklyn. Carrying top weight, which reached 136 pounds in the Brooklyn, he accomplished something that no horse had ever been able to do. In his last race, the Pimlico Special, he had virtually no opposition, and making his own pace he ran the fastest special ever seen on the Pimlico track.

One of the most sensational horses of recent times was a big gray called Native Dancer. He had an enormous stride that measured twenty-five feet at top speed—the same as Man o' War's, which was said to be the longest ever seen on our tracks. Unbeaten as a two-year-old and winning all his races impressively, he was odds-on favorite for the Derby. Blocked and in close quarters early in the race, his stretch drive failed to overhaul front-running Dark Star by a nose. A stride past the finish he was in front. From then on he was unbeaten—usually unchallenged. When an injury forced his retirement he was undisputed champion. He was a great horse—perhaps much greater than we have realized.

There have been many fine horses: Swaps, the Derby winner from California, and his archrival Nashua, considered by the veteran trainer "Sunny Jim" Fitzsimmons the most powerful stayer he ever trained. Bald Eagle was a splendid Cup horse and Kelso was one of the best.

Then there were the great ones of other days. Those who saw

Hindoo, Sysonby, Hanover, and Domino are gone. And the tracks are so different that comparisons can have no meaning. There is no way of accurately evaluating horses of different eras; possibly not even of different years. Only if they could appear on the same track, all in top condition, might we get the answer. And possibly not even then.

STEEPLECHASERS

Two miles is about as far as our race horses are asked to run, usually much less. The steeplechaser's distance is often three miles, and even more. The Maryland Cup, which is considered the toughest timber course in the world, is at four miles, over twenty-two fences.

There is a great difference between racing over brush and over timber. Over brush the pace is faster, for the upper part of the fence can be brushed through without a fall unless the horse goes in too deep, but timber must be jumped clean. Anything but the lightest tick can throw a horse off stride, and a solid rap can often put him down, particularly over a course like the one in Worthington Valley where the Maryland Cup is run. Here many of the rails are like telephone posts and do not give or break.

Considering the distances and the size of the jumps that must be negotiated under high weights, there is bound to be a difference in the conformation and development between the flat racer and the steeplechaser. The race horse rarely is asked to carry more than 130 pounds, and only then if he is in the top bracket, while a chaser of the same class might have to shoulder 160 pounds or more. As a result he usually has more bone below the knee and hock and a more rugged pastern. The impact of landing over a jump at speed is terrific, and clean, powerful legs are an absolute necessity for a horse racing through the field. Speed so multiplies the force of impact that it would be safe to say that the strain on a horse taking a jump at racing speed, with 140 pounds in the saddle, would be greater than in carrying 200 pounds over the same obstacle at a hunting pace. The point that many spectators miss, the action being so fast, is that the jumper lands on one forefoot only. The whole impact of his weight, plus the speed, makes it a small miracle that the chaser stays sound as long as he does.

In conformation, the most notable characteristic of a horse that has raced over jumps for any length of time is his tremendous depth through the girth line, or, as horsemen say, through the heart. It is often so great that it makes him look light-waisted. The shoulder is also developed to a very noticeable degree, for in addition to galloping power he must have the strength to lift the very considerable weight of the forequarters to the required height. Since the driving power in galloping and jumping comes from behind, the quarters of a jumper are always a picture of bulging, deep-grooved power.

Steeplechasing was originally just what the name indicates, a race across country to a church steeple, which made a clear landmark in the green English countryside. These impromptu races were usually staged after a fine run to hounds, with the encouragement of many a glass or tankard of cheer; consequently, they were usually run by moonlight. With such uncertain light and possibly a slightly uncertain seat, many a bedraggled rider arrived at home on foot.

At first steeplechasing was almost entirely limited to hunters, as they were the only horses trained to this pastime. As time went on and the sport grew in popularity, better and faster horses were trained over the jumps and the pace increased. Time was first taken in the Maryland Cup in 1899, and it was more than four minutes behind our present-day course record! That these were only hunters, and very slow hunters at that, is very clear. If raced today, they would have been much more than a mile behind.

Our great chasers have been Thoroughbreds, not quite up to the pace required for flat racing, but nevertheless having a high turn of speed, as judged in this sport. Strangely enough, some sprinters found lacking in stamina on the flat have been able to stay at the slightly slower pace over jumps, and therefore win at distances far beyond their range on the track.

Another unusual quirk is that horses that have been all but unmanageable on the track have made good dependable jumpers. Perhaps they like the grass underfoot; possibly the variety of galloping for a burst and then having a jump come up appeals to them. Years ago, a horse named Billy Barton turned so sour and tough that he was ruled off the track. Put to hunting, and eventually to brush and timber racing, he was sensational. In his first start in the Maryland Cup he fell but was remounted, and in spite of this mishap, won, breaking the course record by more than twenty-three seconds. When remounted, the reins were all on one side of his head and he went across the finish line that way.

Later, sent to England for the Grand National, he looked the certain winner coming in to the last fence, but fell. He was remounted and finished a close second. He did not have smooth sailing over the hazardous course. A horse in front of him made a bad jump at the Canal Turn and landed on top of the fence, where he hung suspended. Billy Barton, hemmed in by other horses, had no choice, so he put in a tremendous leap to clear both the fence and the struggling horse. Undoubtedly this terrific effort took its toll and cost him the race.

Jolly Roger was a star of the first order in the days when steeplechasing was at its height. He was sensational in appearance as well as in performance. A huge, powerful fellow, standing a

Good form over brush; jumping at full speed with just enough clearance.

full seventeen hands, he had more white than any horse that comes to mind. His legs were white well up to the knees and hocks and his blaze covered half of his face. He disproved the old saw about "four white feet and a white nose" with a vengeance, for he won more than any chaser of his day.

Battleship, a small son of Man o' War, accomplished what no other American horse had succeeded in doing, though many had tried. So placed on the rail that he had to face Bechers Brook, that nightmare of hazards, where the turn is sharpest and the drop greatest, he came on to win in unusually fast time. He looked so small against those big, rangy English chasers that he was called "The American Pony." But he had a heart as big as his body and no fence was too much for him.

Another son of Man o' War, Blockade, was the first horse to win the Maryland Cup three times, and in doing so set a new course record. He had such speed that he dominated timber racing until his tragic death in the Virginia Gold Cup. His trainer Janon Fisher said of him, "I rarely schooled Blockade over the jumps. He didn't need it, he knew his business so well. We just galloped him to get him fit. It was no use to school him over small fences; he had no respect for them and got careless. He needed a big fence and a good pace so he could stand back at them. If a horse came into a fence with him, head and head, he usually came down, for few horses could stand back so far and jump so big.

"One day we had him in the paddock; it was a few days after he had won the Grand National, and he was really feeling good. He tore around the paddock a few times and then came down to this corner wide open. He jumped diagonally where the two paddocks met. The fence was five feet high and he really had to get up to clear both fences. The ground was soft enough to clearly

The water jump commands respect. Horses rarely make a mistake here.

show the hoof prints and we measured it. From take off to landing was forty-one feet! If I hadn't seen it I would never have believed it."

Asked how he accounted for such amazing jumping ability he said, "Of course all the Man o' Wars are natural jumpers, but in Blockade I think it was partly his eyesight. He had the clearest eye of any horse I ever saw; just like a crystal. Nothing ever escaped him. He would stop to look at something so far away that you had to look twice to see it. Of course he was a natural jumper, but I believe it was his eyesight that made him able to measure his jumps so accurately and jump so big."

It would seem that galloping at a fast pace and jumping big fences would be more arduous than racing on the flat, and a horse sent to the race track would welcome the change, for he would have much shorter distances to cover and no obstacles, but often this is not so. A handsome dark brown horse named Ossabaw had worked out on the flat at a mile and a half in 2:30, time not often equaled in stakes in that day. The late Louis B. Mayer, hearing of this, bought him. His thought was that, put to flat racing, Ossabaw could win the Santa Anita Handicap.

Ossabaw had great spirit, courage, a dark smoldering eye, and a mind of his own. He hated the race track. They got him into the starting gate for his first start, but never again. He won, but that was it. Soon the riders were afraid to mount him, let alone get him near the starting gate. At last they had to give up and send him East. Back at his own game, racing over the jumps, he was again himself. It was harder work but that was what he liked.

To sum up, a steeplechaser must have almost the speed of a race horse on the flat, a leap in him like an open jumper's that he can use at speed, and great stamina. Since he has to take falls from time to time, he must also have courage of the highest order, for a horse that becomes timid at his fences is useless in this game. There are not many that can be so accurate in measuring their jumps that they do not make an occasional mistake. Only the great Elkridge was all but infallible. In 109 races he fell but twice. That is a record, over a long career, which is little short of miraculous. Every few years the overenthusiastic profess to see another Man o' War in some new sensation that appears on the track. Many, of course, turn out to be just another horse. But nothing has shown up that prompts the most enthusiastic spectator to see another Elkridge. There was just one of him.

JUMPERS AND JUMPING

There are many different opinions on the proper form for jumping, but this difference is mostly in minor details. Hardly anyone now believes in the old form, as shown in old English sporting prints, of sitting back on the horse's loins, with the feet thrust far forward. The *forward seat* has changed all that. With modifications it is almost invariably used in the show ring and hunting field. It is also seen, in an intensified form, in racing over jumps, since the pace is so much faster. The principle of the forward seat is that the rider should be well over the horse's withers when he takes off, leaving his quarters free. The horse can carry weight over the jump much more easily if it is over his shoulders. The same principle is responsible for the jockey's seat on the track, in an even more extreme form because of the great pace.

It goes without saying that your performance should be fairly good at the trot, canter, and gallop before you try jumping. Lack of confidence on the rider's part may cause a horse to refuse the smallest of obstacles, for he can sense your slightest uncertainty. You may fool yourself by putting on a bold front, but you will never fool your horse, so do not try to jump until you can approach the obstacle with eager anticipation and no trace of timidity.

A refusal at the start can be very disconcerting for the beginner and can even cause a fall if he hasn't a strong seat, so start with a small fence that you feel sure the horse will not refuse. A natural jump, such as a low barway between two fields, or brush piled in a narrow path, will almost invariably be taken eagerly and smoothly. The exhilaration of a few such fences will have the beginner well on his way to being a bold rider.

There is a saying that a bold horse makes a bold rider, and it is truer than most. There was a famous hunter years ago that was outstanding in both the hunting field and show ring. He was hunted regularly for ten years over a country that was noted for its big fences and walls, and he was down only twice. Even a timid rider might be bold with such a horse under him. If you can be mounted on a good, willing jumper your confidence will grow with the experience of fine performance. Falls are bound to come to anyone who jumps, but if you can get a lot of gay, perfect jumps under your belt before you have your first fall you will take it in stride. It is seldom as fearful as it looks.

Confidence in both horse and rider is absolutely essential to good performance and this is built up by jumping small obstacles. In a famous Italian cavalry school it was the practice to keep the jumps only a foot high for the first six weeks, and these were no mere beginners. Most had hunted and ridden steeplechasers, yet their training was the same, for absolute perfection of form was the goal.

In jumping, all exponents of the forward seat say the body should be even farther forward than in galloping—particularly at the take-off and over the jump. If you are not you may be *left behind*—the cardinal sin in jumping, for you come down hard on the horse's back and, being off balance, are bound to jerk his mouth. The experts insist that the rider must be merely close to the saddle, not only over the jump, but on the approach and after landing.

Most of a horse's propelling power comes from the hind legs, the forelegs acting chiefly to raise the forequarters to the required height. To use the driving power of his hind legs to best advantage he must have his hocks well under him at the take-off. If he is going too fast he may jump out of a long stride and not get the necessary drive to his jump. You will notice that the high and broad jumpers at track meets always shorten the last stride to get the ultimate amount of spring. When a horse approaches a jump at the right pace and shortens his stride to get into his jump properly, he is *collected*, and will always have "a spare leg," as horsemen put it, ready for any emergency.

Horses vary in their way of jumping. Some jump well from almost a standstill; others need speed to clear an obstacle of any size. If your horse jumps best at speed, it will be necessary to restrain him slightly when he is half a dozen strides from the fence, then give him his head. Otherwise he may be too extended at the take-off and give a sprawling jump, just the opposite of a collected one. Getting in too close to the fence is also awkward, for the horse usually puts in a very short stride and bucks over, with the rider usually left behind. So for a smooth, pleasant performance it is wise to judge your pace so you come into your fences just right.

When a horse jumps he extends his neck and lowers his head, so for full freedom it is necessary to give him plenty of rein. The fact that the rider's body goes forward on take-off provides this slack to some extent, but the rider should always be ready to let more rein slip through his fingers if the horse should peck on landing. Once the horse is in the air, the only thing the rider can do to help is not to interfere with him in any way. If you can hold him into the jump and feel he is not going to refuse, then give him his head, you are apt to get the best performance. *Lifting a horse over the fence*, a phrase sometimes used, does not really say much. A strong, experienced rider can hold his mount to the course and drive him strongly enough so that he will not refuse, but any lifting is done by the horse.

Good form over the jumps. The rider is well forward over the shoulders, where a horse can best carry weight, and is giving her mount enough freedom of the head to perform smoothly.

It is of utmost importance to go into a jump straight, not diagonally, for that can be very dangerous. When you have chosen the spot in the fence you intend to jump, hold your horse to it and do not let him swerve and take it at another point. A horse that gets in the habit of doing this can endanger other riders in a hunting field. Try to be bold at your fences, for any uncertainty you may have is immediately communicated to your horse and almost certainly will bring a refusal. The old saying, "Throw your heart over the fence and the horse will follow," is a very true one. Never stop jumping after a refusal. If necessary, lower the jump, but be sure he has not been left with the idea in his mind that he got away with disobedience. That can be the beginning of a habit which can completely spoil a horse.

If your horse is inclined to get in too close to his jump he will not give the free-flowing action that is so delightful. It often helps to teach a horse to stand back by widening the jump on the take-off side. Brush piled up in front of the jump will make it necessary for him to stand back, and possibly train him to do so.

It is hard to know what you are doing on a horse in action, and often bad habits are acquired unconsciously. If you can have movies taken of you at various paces, and particularly over a jump, you may discover riding faults that you can correct. The better your form, the more smoothly you will ride, and the greater pleasure you will get from riding. The right way is the easiest and most graceful, for there is nothing stilted or artificial about correct riding.

Jumping differs with the type of performance wanted. The *open jumper* of the show ring often has a style quite different from that of the hunter. Unlike the hunter, he is never faulted on form; performance alone counts. Some go so fast that they would be thrown out of consideration over an outside course, where a steady, even pace is required. Some come almost to a stop at each fence, but so long as they go "clean" they can choose their own pace.

A hunter, on the other hand, should go at an even pace, taking his fences in stride. A "good hunting pace," as it is called in the rule book, is a hand gallop; faster than a canter, it is a pace that can be maintained over a distance of ground. The judges vary in their idea of pace; some like more speed than is usual in the hunting field; *going brilliantly*, they term it. If you are showing, it is well to try to find out what the judge's preference is.

Probably everyone is familiar with the seat of the jockeys shown in photographs of Becher's Brook in the Grand National, with the riders lying back so that their backs are almost resting on the horse's quarters, and the feet stuck straight out. Exponents of the forward seat have been loud in criticism of this unorthodox position, but they fail to take into consideration the terrific drop encountered in the Grand National, over a fence higher than any elsewhere. The prime consideration is to stay aboard—no easy feat, since most of the horses peck on landing.

For perfect form watch the military teams in the big horse shows. Here you will never see anything amiss. The heels will be down, the balance perfect, the hands with just the right contact with the mouth. These are the real pros. If you try to emulate them you can't go far wrong.

CARE OF THE HORSE

If a horse is kept in a roomy box stall he will be far better off than in the old-fashioned straight stall. It should be large enough so that he can lie down stretched out. Twelve feet by twelve is a good size, for then he has room enough to move around if he is kept in by bad weather. A clay floor is best, far better than plank or cement. It drains well and will not be apt to cause bruises to knees or hocks if a horse lets himself down where bedding is scant. Such a floor is made by digging down to a depth of two feet and filling in with cinders or small stones. Over this is placed eight to twelve inches of clay, well tamped down. This surface will do wonders for a horse's legs. It is the same feeling you get on the yielding turf of the country after walking on pavement. His hoofs in particular will benefit, for you seldom find dry, shelly hoofs on a horse whose stall has a clay floor.

Water should always be available for him and often replenished, as he cares no more for lukewarm drinking water than you do. A salt block should also be fastened to the wall. He will lick it freely and it will increase his thirst, and plenty of water is important to the health of a horse. A rack is usually used for hay, but there are many horsemen who prefer to have their horses take their hay from the floor. They feel that this is the natural position for feeding, approximating the way a horse grazes, and that it is good for the neck and shoulder muscles.

Hay should be greenish in color, not yellow or brown, and be very fragrant. A horse's sense of smell is very keen and much of the pleasure in his food comes from it. If it is cut at the right time and cured properly you will be well aware of it, for there are few odors so delightful as a stable full of good hay. A horse can be kept in better condition on fine hay alone than on poor hay and plenty of grain.

A horse that is doing six to ten miles a day under saddle will need from six to eight quarts of grain daily. Although the bulk of his feed is oats, there should also be a few handfuls of bran mixed with it and a little corn is also good. Many feed companies put up a horse feed in which oats, corn, and bran are mixed; it is a well-balanced feed and much relished by horses. A clean feedtub is a pretty sure indication that you are not overfeeding, for a horse is a good judge of how much he needs. Many race horses are given as much grain as they will eat; sometimes as much as twelve quarts a day.

If you turn a horse out to pasture a part of each day, he will keep in better condition. Grass is his natural food, his only food in a wild state, and it is to him what salad and green vegetables are to us. If you can arrange to have a door of his stall open onto his pasture, and the door left open, it would be best. When flies are bad he can decide for himself whether he wants to go inside, away from the worst of these stinging pests. Possibly it also gives him pleasure to feel that he is his own boss about some things.

Grooming is to a horse what a daily shower or bath is to you, so it must not be neglected. There should always be a shine to his coat. A few minutes with a body brush will do this. If he has not been too careful of where he has lain down, water and a rag will do a better job than a currycomb and be less irritating to him. A stiffer brush, called a Dandy brush, will keep the mane and tail clean and silky.

"No foot, no horse" is an old English saying, the truth of

which horsemen know only too well. If there is the slightest lameness in any foot a horse is useless. For that reason careful cleaning of the hoofs is very essential, for it is only then that you can see if anything has lodged in the frog. A sharp stone can lame a horse and a nail could be serious.

A horse should be taught early to pick up each hoof on command, but many are not. Since he has a big edge in size and strength it is best not to try to use force. It would be better to follow the advice of the great cavalry leader Xenophon, who wrote in his book on horsemanship: "He will receive the bit more readily if some good should come of it every time he received it." If that doughty warrior was not averse to a bit of bribery, we may well follow suit. Once a horse realizes he will be rewarded if he lifts his hoofs on command, the problem is solved and the cost is not high.

Since the condition of a horse's hoofs is so important, all precautions are useful. A can of neat's-foot oil or black oil and a small brush are most helpful. If the hoof and frog are painted over with this, it will help keep them soft, and it will be especially beneficial to a horse that has to travel over hard or stony roads. It is the dry shelly hoof that develops a crack which makes a horse lame.

He should have plenty of bedding in his stall. In the winter he should be bedded deep, particularly if he is along in years. This can ward off rheumatism and stiffness in the joints and add years to his usefulness. Straw is most commonly used, but fine shavings, if available, make an even drier bed, being so absorbent.

When leading a horse always keep one hand against his shoulder; then if something startles him and he shies, you will move with him and not chance having your foot stepped on. If you

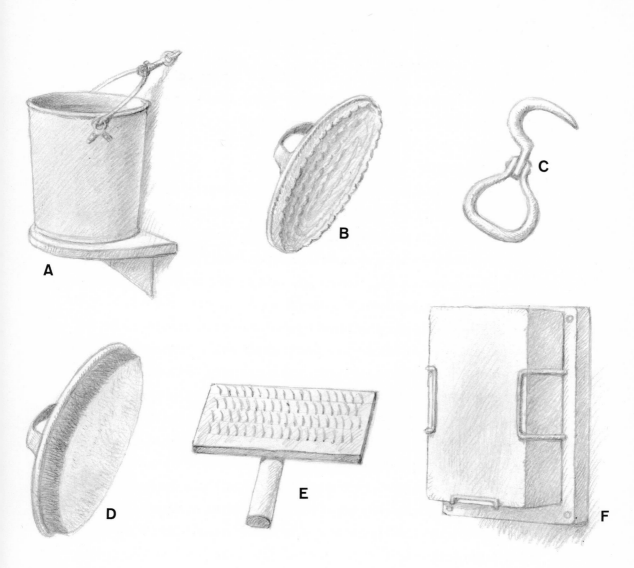

A. Fresh water should always be available to a horse. This arrangement prevents the bucket being tipped over and knocked about.

B. A rubber currycomb does a good job and does not annoy the horse.

C. A hoof pick is necessary to keep the hoofs clean.

D. A good body brush is essential for that well-groomed look.

E. This type of comb does an excellent job on mane and tail.

F. A salt block fastened to the wall of the stall insures that the horse can get all the salt he needs.

have ever had the misfortune of having a horse accidentally tread on you, no one need tell you that this is important. Also remember that a horse is used to being handled from the left, or near, side, even when led. Horses are creatures of habit and dislike any change in routine.

A horse released in pasture is full of enthusiasm and sometimes tries to leave before the lead shank is unsnapped. If he does he may take you, or at least the lead shank, with him. Always see that he is turned facing you before you release him; never turned away. With such a big, powerful animal you must always have everything in your favor if you can.

Catching a horse in an open pasture is a hopeless job if he has other ideas, but if he knows there is always a reward when he comes to your call things are much simpler. Be sure there is always a reward, and what he considers an adequate one. Several pieces of sugar or a couple of carrots will soon have him come galloping to your whistle.

One of the most important rules in the care of horses is never to make a sudden move. Do everything slowly and be sure he sees you. To make a sudden grab at the halter when he approaches you in pasture may well leave you on foot for that day. Reach out slowly and pat him first, then gradually take hold of the halter. Don't let him feel he has been caught.

When you get him to the stable it is best to cross-tie him for grooming. Do not have ropes so short that he cannot reach his shoulder or chest for an annoying fly, merely short enough to keep him in position. Move him slowly when you turn him around and try to avoid having him bump into anything, for this makes a horse very nervous. If anything should happen remember that one "Easy" is worth a dozen "Whoas." A good horseman rarely raises his voice with a horse.

When working around a horse it is a good idea to keep one hand on his body so he always knows where you are. When you walk behind him take a hold of his tail; if he is at all inclined to kick, a strong downward pull is good protection against it. Many horses kick nervously if they sense anything behind them, so be sure to let him know where you are at all times.

It is a good idea to keep in reserve the thing your horse likes best. All horses like carrots and sugar, with sugar usually the favorite. If this is given only for good behavior he will associate it in his mind with obedience. Always offer it to him on a wide-open palm, or he may nip your fingers painfully in his eagerness.

If a horse becomes nervous never let a hint of panic come into your voice. The more upset he is the quieter your voice should be in trying to calm him. Needless to say you should try not to feel any nervousness yourself. Fear has an odor and a horse can smell it.

Undoubtedly the horse is the most conservative of animals, for he likes a regular routine and looks askance at change. He wants to be in a rut. If he does a thing twice he is well on his way to forming a habit. It is well to remember this, for with horses a habit is formed quickly and eradicated slowly. If there are several horses in a stable it is well to feed them in the same order each day. They will resent any change. Never bother a horse while he is eating his grain, for even the gentlest of them might nip or kick. This is the high point of his day; let him enjoy it quietly.

Because horses are large many people pat them with solid whacks, not far removed from punishment. A gentle caress gets much more response, especially around the head. The legendary James Rarey used gentle hands and a quiet voice to cure outlaws in a matter of hours. His advice was to stroke a horse's head as gently as if you were stroking a hummingbird.

Some of the grooms at the tracks and on the breeding farms get amazing response from the horses in their care. Perhaps the reason is that they talk to them a great deal; not just monosyllables, but the same sort of conversation they would carry on with another person. Anyone who has been around horses knows that they like to be talked to and seem almost to understand what is said. The tone of voice is an important consideration. Their understanding need not be limited to "Whoa," "Back," and "Giddap," if you have enough patience to teach them. In 1840 an instructor in languages named Powell performed amazing feats in taming wild horses in a matter of hours and without resorting to force. One of his precepts was that you should talk to your horse and always let him hear the sound of your voice, whether in English, French, Greek, or Latin. Most of us would not have such a range of languages to choose from, but there is one rule we can follow. The horse is a dignified animal. Tell him he is a fine fellow in good English—not baby talk.

AILMENTS

There is an old saying that a veterinary has to be smarter than an ordinary doctor, for he must do his diagnosing without help from his patient. It is true he cannot ask the horse what is the matter, but if he is experienced there are enough signs so that spoken language is unnecessary. A dull coat, listlessness, failure to clean up his feedtub, all will give a clue to what is wrong, if there is enough understanding. The slightest favoring of a leg may well be the first sign of serious lameness. If you wish to be a real horseman no detail should escape your attention. You should know how your horse feels as well as if he could speak to you.

Of all ailments, the most common, and often the most serious, is lameness, for without four sound legs under him a horse is useless. The slightest nodding as he goes along is the first indication. A horse always moves his head up and down to the rhythm of his walk, but if he has pain in a leg his head will come lower when he puts weight on that leg. Heat always develops at the spot of the trouble, so if you feel his leg, starting at the pastern and working upward, you can often determine what is hurting him. A stone bruise will cause heat in the pastern and coronet. A bad job of shoeing can also cause lameness in the pastern, so be sure to get the best blacksmith possible, regardless of cost. He will prove cheapest in the end.

An improperly cleaned stable, where a horse has to stand in wet manure, can cause thrush. This is inflammation in the cleft of the frog. It leads to decay of the frog and in extreme cases the whole frog may rot away. The blacksmith must cut away all the decayed areas. There are various remedies for treating the frog but an old-fashioned one is very effective. Salt is dissolved in vinegar, and painting the hoof with this daily for a week or two will usually clear up the trouble.

Another foot ailment, and a much more serious one, is ringbone, a bony enlargement on the pastern, just above the hoof. If not hereditary it is usually caused by a blow or the jar on the pastern from too much work on hard roads. It will make a horse uncertain in his gaits, inclined to stumble, and in severe cases unfit for use. It is definitely an unsoundness and a serious one; you should never buy a horse with any trace of it.

Laminitis is an inflammation in the wall of the hoof that will put a horse in great pain, often barely able to move about. It is usually caused by too much work when a horse is not in condition, too much water when he is hot and exhausted, or too much grain and not enough exercise. A horse suffering from laminitis will move very painfully, almost walking on his heels.

A splint is a fairly common ailment and not too serious. It is a bony growth on the inside of the foreleg. It may make a horse lame when it first develops but after it has set, or hardened, it will give no trouble. It is usually caused by too much galloping on hard ground or by a blow. It is generally considered a minor blemish, not an unsoundness.

A curb is a thickening of the tendon at the back of the hock a few inches below the point of the hock. It is usually caused by overstrain but will not incapacitate the horse if too much is not asked of him.

Bog spavin is a puffy swelling on the inside and slightly to the front of the hock joint. It is not too serious an ailment and it seldom causes lameness. Bone spavin, a bony growth on the inside of the leg just below the hock, is also a minor ailment caused by strain. If rest does not alleviate it, firing or blistering will usually effect a permanent cure.

A quarter crack is a crack in the wall of the hoof, usually near the center of the hoof. It is most often found on the race track, for it is caused by the strain on the hoof of a horse galloping at top speed. For a complete cure it is necessary for the hoof to grow, so that all trace of the crack disappears as the hoof is cut down. Since a horse often has to grow an entire new hoof before he is again sound, it is a rather serious ailment.

Windgalls are small swellings above the fetlocks, most often on the inside of the cannon bone. They are not a cause of lameness and are merely unsightly.

Stringhalt is classed as a nervous disease and shows itself by the horse picking up one hind leg very high, as if in a reflex action over which he has no control. It is most noticeable when he first comes out of the stable, then gradually diminishes as he goes along. Although there is no cure for it, a horse often retains his usefulness despite it.

A capped elbow, commonly called a shoe boil, is usually caused by a horse striking his elbow with the heel of his forefoot as he lies down. Often the trouble is that the horse is not bedded deep enough and as a result comes down too hard. This causes inflammation and swelling that can be as large as an apple. In extreme cases it will make a horse lame, for it can be as sore as a human boil. In such cases a vet should be called in to lance it. After that it would be wise to strap on a shoe-boil boot to prevent further bruising of the elbow. A capped hock is a similar ailment, again usually due to insufficient bedding on a hard floor. Both ailments are unsightly rather than serious.

When a horse has worms they show up in his manure and he will be thin and in poor condition regardless of the feed he receives. There are various remedies depending on a horse's age and other considerations, so it is best to call in a veterinary.

A bowed tendon is caused by overstrain, usually at high speed, and is therefore more common on the race track than in the riding stable. When a horse bows, the tendon in a foreleg pulls away from the sheath, which causes lameness to a marked degree, for it is painful to put weight on that leg. Blistering and rest may effect a partial cure, but a horse that has bowed is rarely up to hard work afterwards.

A horse is touched in the wind if he makes a deep roaring noise when galloping and shows distress after a short run. This ailment is caused by overexertion when a horse is out of condition. Whistling is a milder form of the same ailment. Some horses blow harder than others after a fast gallop but this does not indicate that they are unsound. There is a definite wheezing sound that the horse makes if touched in the wind.

Colic is a dangerous ailment, for it can strike suddenly and violently and is sometimes fatal if not relieved promptly. It is caused by stoppage of the intestines, followed by a gas formation that presses against the heart. When a horse suffers an attack of colic he will lie down and groan, look toward his body, which will be bloated, and show evidence of great pain. It is wise to have on hand a good colic medicine, for delay can be fatal. Since the horse will be down and weak from pain, it is not difficult to administer. Hold the horse's mouth open and pour the medicine from a test tube as far back on the tongue as possible.

If a horse has a cold it is shown by a discharge from the nose; often his eyes are also running. A horse is more susceptible to

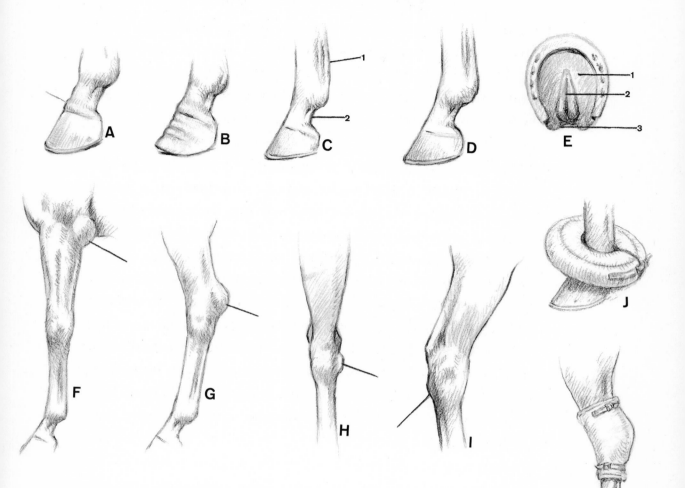

A. Ringbone
B. Laminitis
C. 1. Bowed tendon   2. Pastern that is too short
D. Good pastern for a hack or hunter
E. 1. Wall of the hoof   2. Frog   3. Heel
F. Capped elbow or shoe boil
G. Capped hock
H. Bog spavin
I. Curb
J. Shoe-boil boot is protection against a capped elbow.
K. Hock boot is protection against a capped hock.

pneumonia than man, so be careful to protect him from drafts. Often constipation accompanies a cold. A horse's manure is a good indication of his health and digestion, so notice any departure from the normal. If a physic is needed it is really a vet's job, for giving a horse a pill is not an easy task.

The older a horse is, the more he is subject to illness and ailments. The age of a horse is judged by the teeth, although this method is uncertain after eight or nine. The teeth of a young horse are upright, and slant forward with age. In a young horse's teeth there are small black centers which wear down with age and disappear. At eight these have completely vanished and a horse over eight is said to be aged; the exact age is not given. At this time a groove begins to show in the middle of the teeth at the roots and it extends farther down each year, until at twenty it extends the full length of the tooth. From then on there is no way of telling a horse's exact age, but that is scarcely important, for twenty or less is the span of most horses' lives. Man o' War lived to be thirty, but he was the super-horse in every way, even in longevity.

RIDING TACK AND ITS USE

A good saddle is a prime requisite for enjoyable riding. It must fit the horse's back well and not touch the withers, for a chafe there can be so painful as to make your horse unfit for use. If the horse has a high thin wither it would be best to play safe and use a pad under the saddle. Most horsemen prefer a forward seat saddle which has the flaps cut well forward with a padded knee roll beneath to give the rider added security. This type of saddle is excellent for jumping. The saddle must be thoroughly cleaned and saddle-soaped after each ride. This is particularly important if you ride without a pad, for any dirt that comes in contact with the horse can give him a sore back. The girth should also be kept clean and well soaped since it is in constant contact with the horse. Be sure that your stirrups are large enough for your foot to come free in case of a fall.

It is well for the beginner to learn the correct name for all parts of the riding tack. The front top of the saddle is called the *pommel*; the back, the *cantle*. The straps that hold the stirrups are called *leathers*.

Bridles are of several types, depending on the disposition of the horse. A very quiet mannerly horse can be ridden in a snaffle bridle—one that has only one bit. If that does not suffice when your mount becomes eager or excited, then it would be best to go to the Pelham. This is a single bit with a curb chain and the added curb rein which gives the rider more control of an unruly or over-eager horse. For the horse that is something of a handful, the full double bridle with two bits would be the answer. Be

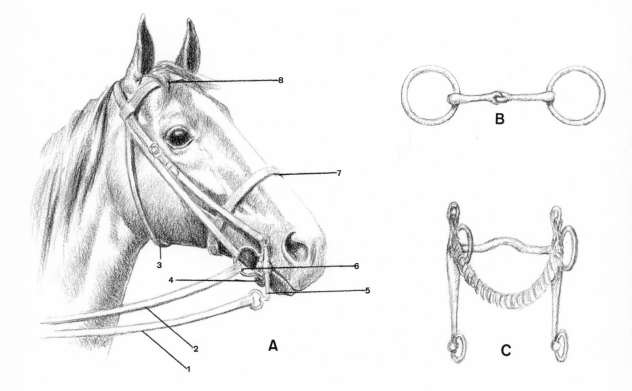

A. A double bridle
   1. Curb rein   2. Snaffle rein   3. Throatlatch   4. Curb chain   5. Curb bit
   6. Snaffle bit   7. Noseband or cavesson   8. Browband
B. Snaffle bit, for a single bridle used on a horse that has a light, responsive mouth
C. Pelham bit, for a horse that does not need a double bridle, but needs a little more than a snaffle

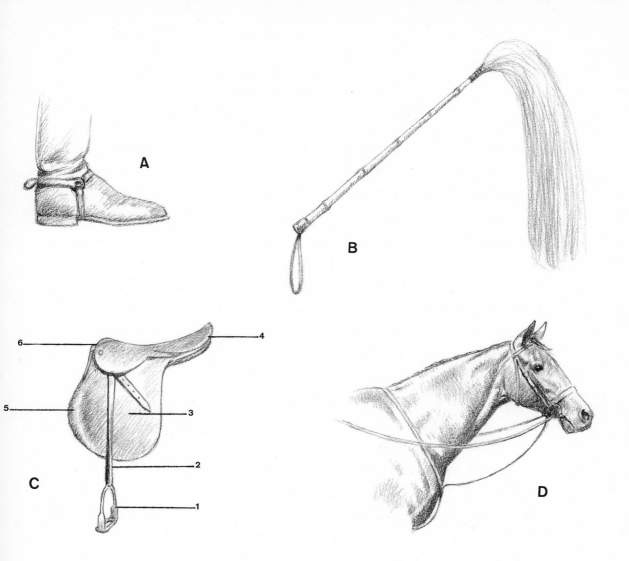

A. A blunt spur such as this can be useful on a sluggish horse; it will be more effective than the heel alone.

B. A fly crop is a great asset to summer riding. With it the rider can keep the horse's head and neck free of annoying flies.

C. The English saddle
   1. Stirrup or iron   2. Stirrup leathers   3. Flap   4. Cantle   5. Knee roll
   6. Pommel

D. A martingale is used to keep a horse from raising his head too high in an attempt to avoid the bit. It is attached to the cavesson and anchored by the girth.

careful to have curb chain lie flat against the groove under the horse's chin; if twisted it can be painful and upset a horse to the point of acting up.

To put a bridle on a horse, throw the reins over his neck before you remove the halter, or you will have no control over him. Place the bit with the thumb in one corner of the horse's mouth and the rest of the fingers in the other. When he feels the bit against his teeth he will usually open his mouth to take it. If he is stubborn about it a reward after he receives it is often effective. When he learns he gets sugar or a carrot as soon as he takes the bit it will present little trouble.

If a horse carries too high a head or throws it up when restrained by the bit, he will probably do better in a martingale. There are two kinds, the standing martingale being the one most commonly used. This is merely a strap attached to the under part of the noseband and going down to the girth to which it is attached by a loop. If adjusted to the proper length it does not interfere with the normal carriage of the head but merely restrains the horse when he tries to get away from the bit. The running martingale, in which the reins run through two rings which are attached by straps to the girth, is used mostly on jumpers, for with it you can give the horse complete freedom of the head and neck in case of a fall or pecking over a jump.

Needless to say, the bit that goes into the horse's mouth should be as immaculately clean as the spoon you put into your own. A horse has a much more sensitive nose than you and possibly a keener palate; so it is wise to see that all his tack is kept clean.

In fly season, a fly crop can be a godsend. With it you can flick the horse's head and neck free from flies, some of whose bites are really venomous. A thin fly sheet for use in the stable when flies are bad is an added comfort.

Shoeing is of utmost importance if a horse is to go well. For the hack or hunter, too long a toe is a disadvantage, for it puts the pastern at too great an angle and can cause stumbling. Generally a horse needs shoeing every five or six weeks. Hoofs are inclined to get dry, particularly if used over hard or stony roads, and it is a good idea to brush them daily with hoof dressing which has an oil base. This can also be used to good advantage on the frog of the hoof, which acts as a cushion and so should be kept soft and resilient.

A hunting crop, with its long lash, can be a very useful part of a rider's equipment if he encounters dogs on his rides, for often a dog dashing out suddenly can upset a horse and a hunting crop makes it easy to keep him at his distance. Also, most horses go more freely if they see their rider is carrying a stick or crop, even if he never uses it.

A good, well-fitted pair of boots is a very important part of the rider's equipment. They should be long enough to reach within a few inches of the kneecap and fit very snugly at that point. This is not only for appearance but it gives a much more secure knee grip, which is so essential in riding. If riding in jodhpurs be sure they fit very closely at the knee and upper part of the calf. This is also essential in riding breeches.

Many horses go better if they know the rider is wearing spurs. If you ride well enough to always keep your heels away from the horse except when urging him on, a blunt spur is useful equipment, particularly for jumping. Such a spur does not hurt a horse but is mildly uncomfortable and he will respond to it more readily than to the heel alone.

RIDING

The most important part of a rider's equipment is the horse. Not just any horse, but one that is willing to move along and do it fairly smoothly at all gaits. Of course, the beginner would not want too much spirit, for to over-mount the novice may bring on a timidity that will never be overcome. But the horse should fulfill George Washington's requirement: "A horse that will go along." A willing disposition comes first, for neither whip nor spur will cure a sullen, ungenerous horse.

In mounting you should stand facing the horse, reins in the left hand, which may also grasp a handful of mane as extra security. Put the left foot in the stirrup, and grasping the saddle with the right hand, spring from your right leg and swing it over into the saddle. This is not as easy as it sounds, especially if you are short and your horse is tall. Usually it is best to resort to the mounting block. Try to ease yourself into the saddle and not come down on it with a bang. That makes a horse more conscious of the fact that he has to carry weight. Once in the saddle it is wise to reach down and feel the girth, for often a horse will swell himself up when the girth is tightened. With weight in the saddle he will relax and you can easily pull up a hole or two if necessary.

The proper length of your stirrups can be determined by placing the stirrup under your armpit and extending your arm along the taut stirrup leather until your finger tips touch the hook to which the leathers are attached. If you find you are constantly losing your stirrups as the horse moves along you can shorten the leathers a hole or two in order to get the pressure to hold the stirrups in place. Be sure the stirrup leathers are the same length or you will be riding lopsidedly and off balance. At first it might be better to ride with the stirrup *home*, that is pushed to the heel rather than on the ball of the foot, for the beginner is always in danger of losing his stirrups. The men who ride jumpers ride with the stirrup home.

Many horsemen stress the importance of keeping the foot on the inside of the stirrup tread so that the sole of the boot is turned slightly outward. This forces the knee into the saddle and makes certain your lower leg is away from the horse and you are not gripping with the whole leg. The grip should be with the thigh, knee, and upper part of the calf. Your heel and ankle should be away from the horse at all times except when used to urge him on. Be sure the stirrup is large enough so that your foot will readily come free in case of a fall. The line of the stirrup leathers should at all times be perpendicular to the ground in both hacking and jumping. A good test to see if you are in balance is to rise in the stirrups. If there is no tendency to fall either forward or backward you are sitting properly.

The old precept to turn the toes in should not be taken literally. Actually you cannot turn the toes in and still keep the knee in position to have a firm grip. If your grip is correct through the thigh and knee, the toe will of necessity be in the right position.

Since the muscles used in riding are different from those exercised in other sports, a beginner is often surprised and discouraged to find how sore and lame he may be after his first rides. Because of his uncertainty he grips harder than will be necessary with more experience, when he will rely more on balance.

The body should be held upright in the saddle, inclined forward enough so the balance of weight is over the stirrups. Be as relaxed as possible so that your body follows the movements of the horse. "Always be *with* your horse" is one of the top precepts in riding. When you are riding in good form no muscle is strained or twisted in an unnatural position, and you should look and feel at ease.

A rider who controls his horse smoothly and well with a minimum use of the reins is said to have good hands. Since a rider who has an uncertain seat will invariably balance himself by the reins, thus putting unnecessary pressure on the bit, it is clear that to have good hands you must have a good seat on a horse. Every ounce of pressure on the reins should be calculated and intentional, never accidental. A rider with bad hands can ruin both a horse's mouth and his disposition.

Holding the reins with both hands is best. Riding with one hand is apt to advance that shoulder and so twist the body slightly off balance. These points may seem trivial, but in riding properly the smallest details are important. It is only by watching all points that you get the ultimate pleasure from the sport. To see a real horseman putting a horse through his paces is a delight. Here are rhythm and coordination raised to the nth degree.

If you are riding with a double bridle, one rein passes outside the little finger and the other inside it, with the thumb controlling the pressure on the reins. The curb rein should be kept slacker than the snaffle, for it is the more severe and should only be brought into play if the snaffle does not suffice. The pressure should be applied gradually, for a sudden jerk can bruise the bars of the mouth. It is in this way that the prized light mouth of a horse is lost. Many people think the bit lies against the teeth but this is not so; it actually fits the tenderest part of the mouth.

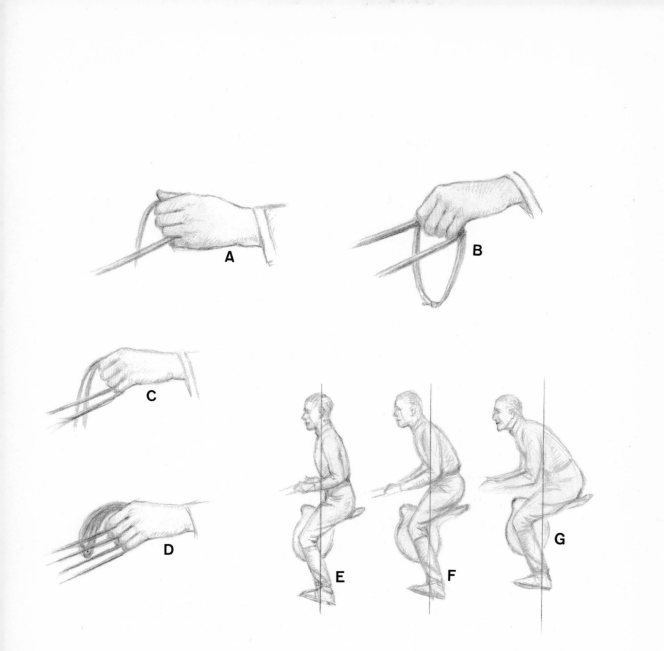

A. Correct way of holding the reins with a snaffle bridle
B. Riding with one hand with a snaffle bridle
C. Correct way to hold reins of a double bridle
D. Riding with one hand with a double bridle
E. The proper balance at a walk
F. The trot calls for more forward inclination of the body.
G. At the canter and gallop there is more weight ahead of the line of
balance than behind it.

Keep your head erect when riding and always look between the horse's ears to see where you are going. Then you can see the road and avoid anything that might cause your horse to stumble and also observe any movement in the ears, for a horse gives his first indications of nervousness or fear there. Often a shy can be anticipated and not be so disconcerting as when there is no warning.

In learning to ride you should make haste slowly. Be patient and remember that the walk comes before the trot, the trot before the canter, and the gallop not at all—at least for the novice. There might be quite an interval between. In this field it does not do to try to skip grades.

After mounting, settle yourself firmly in the saddle—heels pressed strongly down into the stirrups so you are not in danger of losing them. Be sure your knees are firm against the saddle flaps, for this is your security. When you are ready to let the horse move forward, shorten the reins enough to have a light "feel" of the mouth, for even at a walk there should be control and the horse should always be *up to the bit*. A horse ridden on a slack rein, even at a walk, becomes sloppy, and can stumble badly. A walk can be a most pleasant gait if the horse moves smoothly and freely. A little extra pressure with the lower leg and a slight lift of the head will help to keep your mount alert. You must always ride your horse, never be a mere passenger.

Once you are riding smoothly and comfortably at the walk, and feel balance and security in the saddle, you can proceed to the trot. At the trot the horse's forefoot and the hind foot on the opposite side go forward in unison, so it is on a diagonal. Since two of the horse's feet are off the ground at the same time, there is considerable up-and-down movement and it would not be comfortable to try to sit close to the saddle. That is the reason for *posting* to the gait. In posting, as the horse's action throws you forward and upward, by use of your legs you remain up long enough to miss the bump of the next stride. Done smoothly, it makes the trot the most graceful of gaits and perhaps the pleasantest. Your knee grip must be firm enough to fully control the fall of the body; the horse's action gives you the rise. A finished horseman posts so close to the saddle that his rise is hardly perceptible, but a beginner might do well to rise as high as the horse's action throws him in order to get the rhythm clearly in mind. In the trot the body is inclined forward more than at the walk and well-balanced over the stirrups. That balance is absolutely indispensable. Be sure that you have only a light feel of the reins and do not balance by them. A good seat is the best insurance against this. To keep a light touch with the horse's mouth, your hands will move constantly as the head moves. Keep the elbows to the sides; do not flap them up and down. That is awkward and the mark of the rank beginner.

The canter and gallop are really the same gait, but the canter is much slower—a controlled, rocking-chair pace. On a smooth horse it can be the easiest of all paces, for you can sit close to the saddle and relax completely. Many ride it upright and deep in the saddle. Still, the leading exponents of the forward seat maintain that at any pace beyond the trot the back half of the saddle could be cut away and the rider should never miss it.

It cannot be stressed too often that at all paces the saddle leathers should always be perpendicular to the ground, or else the rider's weight is not balanced over the stirrups. As the pace increases, so should your knee grip, but be sure not to grip with the lower part of the leg. The pressure of the ankle and heel is a signal for more speed and if you use it accidentally your horse may get out of control.

When you are far enough along to try a hand gallop be sure

you have a well-cushioned surface, for as the pace increases so does the strain on the horse's legs. Turf is by far the best, and there is something about the feel of it that may reach back into the past, for a horse gallops over it with more joyous abandon than on any other ground.

If you are cantering in a circle be sure your horse is *leading* with the inside foreleg; that is, it is going forward first. This is because only then is he in balance. You can feel the awkwardness when he is on the wrong lead by his uncertainty on the turns. In the show ring you will be severely faulted for this, so always stop him and start again if he is leading with the outside leg.

In restraining a horse that is getting out of hand, a strong knee grip supplementing the reins is a decided asset. It gives him a feeling that the rider is in control. It would be well to have reins cut to such a length that by merely spreading your hands you can let the reins slip through your fingers to shorten them in an instant. If you have a lot of slack this cannot be done, and often the quickness with which you can shorten rein is important. As soon as your mount responds, release pressure, for it is important that he definitely connects punishment with misbehavior.

When hacking on country roads there are a number of things to keep in mind. Never go fast past a house. Many things can happen to cause a bad shy, and a sudden shy can put down any rider if he is unprepared. A door opening suddenly, a dog leaping out unexpectedly can be dangerous. In going on roads where there are cars, ride on the wrong side of the road so that your horse can see cars approaching. In these days few drivers of cars have the slightest knowledge of horses, and neither slow down nor give a horse room enough when coming up behind him. The laws are still on the books that make it imperative for a

Jockeys ride the forward seat, though in a greatly exaggerated style.

car to stop if a man with a horse signals for it, so use it whenever necessary.

The *aids* are what help control the horse: the legs, the hands, the reins, and also the weight and voice. The legs are used mostly to urge the horse forward, but can also be used to turn him to right or left, by pressure of the opposite leg. Thus you can move him slightly to either side to avoid stones in the path without recourse to the reins, which can be reserved for more definite movements. On a high school horse or a gaited saddle horse, the legs as aids play a much greater part in signaling what is desired.

Do not break a horse from a trot to a canter; stop him and, by use of the legs, have him canter from the first stride. If he goes into a canter from the trot it will more likely be a gallop, for the inclination is to speed up, and the canter is no faster than a good trot. Each gait should be separate and on command.

If a horse is disobedient and will not give you the pace you ask for, turn him back and make him go over the same stretch of road time and again until he is bored enough to give what you ask for. When he learns this will be repeated each time he is disobedient he will soon behave.

Be sure to distinguish between fear and acting up in a horse, for if you punish fear you always increase it. No one has ever cured a shying horse by punishment; he has only added fear of punishment to the animal's nervousness. At such times he needs soothing, not the whip. Think in terms of your own nervousness, how little you can do to control it. As one groom said of horses, "They're only human."

HORSEMEN'S TALK

Horsemen have a language all their own. Sometimes it does not quite conform to grammatical rules, but it has color and says what is meant. Often writers of fiction run through all the superlatives and still do not come up with anything as descriptive of courage and stamina as the horsemen's phrase *deep through the heart*.

To the seasoned horseman hardly any horse is perfect. As he will say, "They all have a hole in them somewhere." Many of the terms used to describe faults as well as good qualities are picturesque. Some of these follow.

A horse is always handled and mounted from the left or *near side*. In the old days it was usually known as the *nigh side*. The right is the *off side*.

When a horse is said to be *on the leg* it means he is longer legged than is desired for good conformation.

Herring gutted means that a horse is slack and undeveloped through the loins.

A head and neck are *well set on* when they are in good relation to a sloping shoulder and the head is carried well.

Over at the knee means that the horse stands with the leg bent slightly forward at the knee. Many horsemen do not consider this a fault, such as being *back at the knee*, where the line of the front leg is slightly concave; such a horse seldom stays sound.

Tied in below the knee means that the circumference of the leg just below the knee is less than farther down the leg, which is considered a weakness.

When a horseman says a horse has *plenty of bone*, he judges by the circumference of the cannon bone between the knee and pastern. Eight and a half to nine inches is considered good.

A horse that *makes a noise* is *touched in the wind*, or wind-broken, and is not sound.

One that *dishes* or *paddles* throws his feet out to the side much as the average girl does when running. This is a fault (in a horse).

When a horse *goes short* he is lame, and this is signaled by the up-and-down motion of the head, called *nodding*.

A *free-going horse* is one that goes willingly without urging. More common, especially in riding stables, are those that are *herd bound* or *stable bound*, that is they are unwilling to go out alone or to leave the stable.

A *grass-cutter* or *daisy-cutter* lifts his feet just enough to barely clear the ground.

A horse has *true action* when he moves his legs in a straight line at all times. This can best be seen when standing behind him.

He *carries a good head* when it is up, alert, and responsive to the bit.

A *sloping shoulder*, so much desired, means that the wither is well back so as to allow maximum length to the shoulder blade.

Horsemen prefer *short cannons*, which means that the knees and hocks are low, or *well let down*. This makes for a longer stride.

The *top line* of a horse is the line from the ears, along the neck and back to the tail. It should be a flowing line with a hint of angularity, indicating strength.

A good pair of breeches is old English, or more likely Irish, for a horse with very well-developed quarters, thighs, and gaskins.

Saying a horse *girths big* is the same as the more picturesque phrase *deep through the heart*. Depth through the girth is important, for the heart and lungs are there.

Plenty of bottom means plenty of stamina and ruggedness.

A horse that carries his tail in a high-spirited manner is said to *carry a good flag*. It is a rather apt phrase, since no sluggish or unwilling horse carries a tail that has any resemblance to a flag.

A good horse should have a short back, but still, in the horseman's parlance, should *stand over a lot of ground*. In other words he should be so well developed in the shoulder and quarters that despite the short back he literally does stand over a lot of ground.

Well-sprung ribs can be seen from the front. The *barrel* should be big in diameter.

When a horse has his *feet well under him* he is in perfect balance.

A *heavy-headed* horse is one that makes little or no response to the bit and needs a lot of muscle to control him. His opposite is the one with a *light mouth* that responds to the slightest feel of the reins.

A rider with *light hands* is one who uses the reins with the utmost delicacy and controls the horse with the slightest possible use of the bit. His opposite is the heavy-handed rider who can soon spoil a horse with his pulling and sawing at the reins.

Good clean bone means that the cannon (the bone between the knee and the hock) is free of splints and there is no puffiness between the cannon and the tendon.

A *using horse* is one that is a good performer in harness and also under saddle; in fact, an all-around useful horse.

A horse that is not responsive to the bit and requires quite a bit of strength on the part of the rider is called a *puller*. Horsemen consider this a serious fault.

A jumper that takes his fences with plenty to spare is said to be *jumping big.*

Jumping clean means clearing fences without touching them.

A *peck* is a slight mistake on landing over a jump but not enough to put a horse down.

When a stallion is at stud at a farm he is said to *stand* there. A *season* to a stallion is acquired by payment of the stud fee. A stallion is called *sure with his mares* if they are usually in foal at the first mating.

A stallion is said to *stamp his get* when his offspring inherit his characteristics to a marked degree.

A *brood-mare sire* is one whose fillies are outstanding when they mature and are sent to the breeding farms. Such mares are called *good producers.*

A stallion is said to *outbreed himself* if he sires a horse better than himself.

Inbreeding is mating two individuals closely related in blood. This is seldom done.

An outcross is mating two individuals of entirely different bloodlines.

The race track horsemen have a vocabulary of their own that relates to their calling. It grew over the years and has color and is strongly descriptive.

A *morning glory* is a horse that is sensational in morning work-outs but nothing at all in the afternoon under the stress of real competition. A horse *flattens out* when he fails to respond to the rider's urging. A *good post horse* is one that is quiet and mannerly at the starting gate. A horse that can carry his speed beyond a mile and a quarter is said to *stay* or be a *stayer.*

If a horse weakens the jockey may say, "I called on him but he was empty." A horse is *rated* when he runs against a strong pull in the first part of a race. If he quits, the jockey will say, "He spit out the bit." A horse is *put to a drive* when the jockey calls for all his speed. A *front runner* is one that wants to take the lead from the start. He is usually hard to rate and short on stamina.

Sometimes a horse goes faster in a morning workout than was planned and as a result may not run his true race. Then it is said, "He left his race on the track."

A horse is *rank* when he refuses to respond to his rider and is rough and unruly. *Leaning on the bit* is different. This is an eager horse that wants to do everything asked of him—and maybe a little more. The veteran horseman is conservative and chary of adjectives. What we might call a fine horse is a *nice horse* to him. The one we would call a great horse is only a *good horse*. You will have to wait around a long time to hear him use *great*. Maybe a decade or two.

INDEX

Date Due

JY 22 '65			
JA 22 '66			
FE 25 '66			
MR 19 '68			
4/22/68			
MAY 12 '69			
DE 11 '74			
DEC 6 '84			
FACULTY			
JUL 30 1992			
AUG 09 2002			
AUG 05 2002			